Business and Sales: The Guide to Success as a Personal Trainer

Business and Sales: The Guide to Success as a Personal Trainer

Eddie Lester

© 2016 Eddie Lester
All rights reserved.

ISBN: 1539982866
ISBN 13: 9781539982869
Library of Congress Control Number: 2016918780
CreateSpace Independent Publishing Platform
North Charleston, South Carolina

Do you need Continuing Education Units or Credits?
(CEUs, CECs)

The Business and Sales: The Guide to Success as a Personal Trainer is now available online at www.fitnessmentors.com/business-and-sales-ceu-course/ . Visit the link or call today (424) 675-0476 to reserve your 2.0* CEUs and recertify your personal training certification.

Approved for CECs from the following companies:
NASM, NESTA, ACE, ACSM, NSCA,
AFAA, ISSA, NCCPT

*Number of CECs varies by certifying body.

What You Can Expect to Learn from this Guide

Discipline. It's what got you through all those reps and maintained you through the certification process, and it still drives you to succeed. This guide will lead you through the process of building on—and building up—your personal-training business. It is not just an A, B, C tutorial, nor is it a simple step-by-step how-to manual. This guide will draw on your knowledge as a professional trainer, tap into the discipline that is already inherently a part of you, and provide a pathway for you to get to the next level of business and financial success.

Many trainers attain their certifications and gain a couple of clients, but they find themselves flailing because the personal-training market is saturated and the competition is tough, which makes it easy to get discouraged. You have the training and the education, the know-how and the drive. Now, it's time to turn that into a successful personal-training business.

The first section of this guide covers preparation: it is a review of what certifications are necessary to begin your career. It then helps you define your fitness theory and personal and business branding. This section is very important, as it is an excellent primer on the business of business—establishing a trademark and naming, structuring, and registering your business—and it covers accounting resources and banking tips. Lastly, it covers the many aspects of growing your business using social media.

The next two sections may surprise many readers because both titles contain the word "free": "Give Away Free Information" and "Offer a Free Service". Within these two sections reside excellent information for determining your niche, which is the cornerstone for everything that follows as it is what establishes your target audience. The information contained in these two sections will help you think through what information and services will attract clients to your business and, which of these, if offered for "free," would entice the client to subsequently opt to become a paying client.

The art of the sale is what drives the section called *"Engage the Prospect"*. The previous sections helped define your niche and therefore your target audience. The sections that follow are the meat of this guide and are not for the faint of heart. If you internalize them, these sections can be your compass and help narrow your focus by clearing out the clutter and worry. How to engage the prospect by establishing a hierarchy of engagement and make that first impression and the importance of follow up and outreach. This section also includes sample dialogue and communication ideas for e-mail and text message—the least desirable form—and face to face interactions, which are the most desirable.

"Prove You Care" is the next-to-last section. It seems self-explanatory and simple. However, this section details how to determine your sales personality and gives examples of several of them. It also helps you understand the product you are selling and provides analysis about the psychology of why people buy. This section helps you delve deeper into pinpointing what needs and fitness goals clients have in mind and tells you how to ask questions that will not only assist your clients in clarifying their goals but will subsequently create an emotional connection between you and the client that will bind you together to achieve those goals.

The closing section discusses how to set your prices, discuss pricing with your clients, and structure your pricing to attain financial goals. There are useful tables showing various strategies and scenarios for fitness packages and pricing. As the "Prove You Care" section discussed the psychology of buying, this section goes over barriers that keep potential clients from buying, offers insight into creating solutions, and includes several stories about how the author used questions designed to reveal the barrier, create the solution, and close the sale.

About the Author

With over a decade of industry experience and six years of teaching experience as a college professor, Eddie Lester has used his bachelor of science in kinesiology and more than ten certifications to grow a successful personal-training business. His fitness education company, Fitness Mentors, which assists entrepreneurs looking to start their careers as certified personal trainers, has helped thousands of people turn their passions for fitness into revenue-generating, full-time careers. Eddie is often found at the beach playing volleyball, surfing, and enjoying the salty air with his wife and son.

Contents

Foreword · xiii

Introduction · xvii

Chapter 1   Prepare · 1

   Credentials · 1

   Mastery of Your Craft · · · · · · · · · · · · · · · · · 2

   Your Fitness Theory · · · · · · · · · · · · · · · · · · 2

   Branding · 5

   Business Checkpoints · · · · · · · · · · · · · · · · 7

   Social Media · 13

Chapter 2	Give Away Free Information · · · · · · · · · · · · · · · 18	
	Determine Your Niche · · · · · · · · · · · · · · · 18	
	Target Your Niche · · · · · · · · · · · · · · · · · · · 20	
	Create Opt-In Opportunities · · · · · · · · · · · 22	
	Bonus Opt-In Strategies · · · · · · · · · · · · · · · 25	
Chapter 3	Offer a Free Service · 36	
	Decide What Services Will Attract Your Niche · 36	
	Create Your Atmosphere · · · · · · · · · · · · · · 38	
Chapter 4	Engage the Prospect · 41	
	Hierarchy Of Engagement · · · · · · · · · · · · 42	
	Your First Impression · · · · · · · · · · · · · · · · · 44	
	The Follow-Up · 47	
	Continued Outreach · · · · · · · · · · · · · · · · · 50	
Chapter 5	Prove You Care · 52	
	Your Selling Personality · · · · · · · · · · · · · · · 52	
	What Product are you Selling? · · · · · · · · · 55	

	Why People Buy	57
	What Does the Client Want or Need?	63
	Power Questions	67
Chapter 6	Close the Sale	73
	Setting Your Prices	73
	Discussing Pricing	77
	Picking a Pricing Structure	79
	Identifying Reasons People Don't Buy	85
	Identifying Barriers and Creating Solutions	86
	Sales Stories	89
	Creating Closing Sales Statements	91
	Being Sure Clients Don't Leave Without Your Help	95
	Conclusion	97
	References	99

Foreword

There is a tragic archetype in fitness. Time and time again, we see bright coaching minds that are making critical impacts on the well-being of others who cannot support themselves with their craft. I'm troubled by imagery of world-class weightlifting coaches sitting sloppily in fold-out chairs in dingy gyms. It's always that folding chair. The scene never fairly describes the value of what's between the coaches' ears. A coach, who is old now, is equal parts an endless well of training expertise and a person who is calloused by the underappreciation of his or her work. While these coaches know how to make numbers grow on the barbell, they rarely know how to do the same with their bank statements. In fact, the disparity between coaching mastery and success in business often turns into a source of prideful martyrdom. With dusty old photos of past Olympians and athletes on podiums strewn along the walls, these fitness gurus take an us-against-the-world approach that can go as far as saying that being a marketable authority in the fitness space with a viable business is something for quacks and industry posers.

It's not.

In fact, I'm here to tell you that the prideful suffering of brilliant trainers need not continue. What's more, it's time for us coaches and trainers to buck up and realize that there are no martyrs. When you become a trainer, you get the opportunity to delve into a passion—for changing health, teaching movement, or offering a service to others—but you also become a businessperson by default. Pretending otherwise is a lie and is a surefire way to dissolve your ability to act on your aforementioned passions. Your duty to master your craft with knowledge of the body, training stimuli, and techniques is tethered to a duty to be successful in business. Consider your inability to develop a business that operates profitably, for example, as just as critical a failure as not being able to cue squatting mechanics.

Your people need you to be successful. After all, it's the successful trainer that can influence more positive change in more people. It's the successful trainer that creates access to better facilities, develops and attracts more excellence, and is a devoted professional. As in any craft, part-timers rarely outperform full-time professionals. Furthermore, trainers that can't make livings can't train. Not only is it okay to be successful, you must be successful to live your passion.

When it comes to the full-time professional, Eddie Lester is on my short list. In the many years I've known him, it's his recognition of coaches' dualistic responsibilities that excites me most. We must be masters of our craft, as he will tell you, but we also must organize our mind-sets to address the second half of our profession's responsibility. This text is a breath of fresh air. Its importance can't be underscored too much as there is no shortage of opportunities for coaches to learn about movement. What coaches need are the skills to have a chance to teach movement for years to come. Despite some misconceptions, those skills rarely relate to the movements of the scapula.

Luckily, fitness is a positive environment, but simply being in it isn't enough to keep your training business alive. As my friend, fellow strength and conditioning coach and ten-year NFL veteran, John Welbourn says, "No one is coming to save you." At least with this text, you have a chance to save yourself. When it comes to the business side of training, I need you to try, your clients need you to try, and, above all, your livelihood demands that you try.

Logan Gelbrich

Introduction

There are almost three hundred thousand certified trainers in the United States, making the personal-training (PT) field very competitive. With so many people trying to muscle their ways into the industry, it is important to find your corner of the PT market and create a successful business for yourself. Although the field is filled with people with the best of intentions—to promote healthy lifestyles while looking one's absolute best—it is also filled with people who falsely believe the industry is an easy one to conquer. In reality, 20 percent of people certified in personal training give up in less than one year because their business effort does not translate into the business success needed to start and maintain a successful enterprise.

This book will define what it takes to build a successful personal-training business, which can lead to both financial freedom and personal fulfillment. Everything discussed, from starting-up and preparing to fine-tuning your sales, will lead to your success as a fitness-business owner.

CHAPTER 1
Prepare

Credentials

The most successful personal trainers are not necessarily the most knowledgeable. Some trainers are successful because they connect with people and motivate them or because they have proven track records. Other trainers are successful solely because they have the nicest bodies they have ever seen. Whatever method is used to motivate clients, the common thread for any successful personal trainer is the possession of a nationally recognized certificate proving knowledge in the personal-training field.

Completion of a certificate program from a certifying body that is accredited by the National Commission for Certifying Agencies (NCCA), is the first step to any fitness career, as it is required for employment at most gyms across the United States. Companies such as the National Academy of Sports Medicine (NASM), the National Strength and Conditioning Association (NSCA), the American College of Sports Medicine (ACSM), the American Council on Exercise (ACE), and the National Exercise and Sports Trainers Association (NESTA) have taken the necessary steps to create approved education programs for your beginning steps as a personal trainer. Whichever company you choose, it is important to align yourself with an NCCA-accredited certification, as the future of your business depends on it.

Earning extra credentials are like super-setting your two favorite body parts: they not only pump you up (insert Arnold's voice) but also add value to your portfolio of skills and expertise. Be sure to expand your education by taking courses that interest you and apply to your future target market.

Mastery of Your Craft

Your CPT certification was the foundation from which you built your initial confidence, and now, you have a proven, comprehensive training model that will successfully take people to their goals. As your training style has evolved and you have seen your clients meet fitness goals, you have aligned yourself with certain methodologies and created a robust toolbox. And as you have gained confidence and experience in your training methods, your core beliefs about the nature of true health have emerged. Now, your innovative self shall rise out of the muck of repetition, where stability-ball squats and ball dumbbell chest presses reigned supreme. Your style is emerging, and you are the trainer that stands out because you get clients in great shape while doing whatever type of training you do (TRX, BOSU, CrossFit, triathlon, circuit, old-school body building, yoga, etc.). Now is the time to hone those beliefs and make them the focus of your business, which, in turn, will become your sales mantra.

Your Fitness Theory

Selling someone else's fitness theory can be a difficult task, especially if you do not believe in what you are selling. Your fitness theory needs to emerge out of your core beliefs about what true health is. It defines you as a trainer and at the same time becomes your sales pitch. Below are questions to help you recognize your current fitness theory:

1. What is health?
2. What is your daily routine to promote health? Why is this your daily routine?
3. What are forms of exercise or exercise combinations that have worked to get you in the best shape?
4. How and what do you eat? Why?
5. What is the best way to create a new habit or behavior based on your experience? Give an example.

These questions are meant to get you thinking in terms of your product because you are the prime example of why your routine works—and works well. Having these answers in mind is also important in building client relations and then translating your routine—and your belief in it—into results for your clients. And, the answers subsequently form the cornerstone in terms of branding, selling, and marketing products for your business. Below are short example answers to these questions to give you a better idea of how your fitness theory might come about. Do not let these answers below distract you from what you truly believe in.

1. What is health? It is an alignment of physical, mental, and spiritual well-being. Eat well, sleep well, exercise, and pray or meditate.
2. What is your daily routine to promote health? After eight hours of sleep or more, I wake up and prepare breakfast and two lunches simultaneously. This ensures there will always be good food no matter where you go. Upon completing your breakfast, grab a twenty-four-ounce water

bottle and begin binge drinking. Around eleven o'clock, eat your first lunch, which may consist of chicken, a sweet potato, and some green leafy veggies. Following lunch, hit the gym for a quick workout. Once done, have a protein shake and a sweet potato to enhance recovery. Eat your second lunch between two and three o'clock. Prepare a healthy dinner, and unwind from the day. Go to bed early to ensure eight hours or more of sleep, and dream of barbells and weight plates. Why is this a good daily routine? Easy: it will achieve your goals of health and a super sexy bod.
3. What are exercises that have worked to get you in the best shape? Properly periodized three-to-four-week strength programs, with one to twenty reps and short rest periods. (This is a generalization—you should be more detailed.)
4. How do you eat? I eat what nature would provide if I were in the wilderness, jungle, desert, or a coastal community—things with one ingredient. I monitor these foods with IIFYM (if it fits your macros *iifym.com*) and the My Fitness Pal app to determine proper gram quantities and calories to best fit my current goal. (Meal plans and more detail about your nutritional strategies will benefit you, so do not skimp out.)
5. What is the best way to create a new habit or behavior based on your experience? Give an example. (If you are having trouble with this one, use Prochaska's Transtheoretical Model.) Consider having your client work with someone who already has this new habit or behavior in order to learn tips and tricks to best optimize creating said behavior. An example would be to have a client watch you prepare your meals while you explain the new diet he or she will be starting.

Now that you know what you believe in, you can begin to create documents that clearly deliver your message. Types of documents can be programs, nutritional guides, meal plans, behavioral-change strategies, exercise charts, mission statements, slogans, and so forth. Be aware that these documents will be your products, which can be sold exclusive of or in conjunction with your personal-training.

Branding

You have now developed your fitness theory, leading you to a set of principles that govern the direction of your business. It is time to live your life immersed in what you believe. Branding can be looked at in many different ways, but the first step is believing in what you do. Then you must constantly ensure that you live and breathe your new brand.

Personal Branding

The most important type of branding to individual trainers is personal branding. You can get an idea for how you should address your own personal branding by how you answered the question about your daily routine to promote health in the fitness theory section. This type of theory and lifestyle you promote should help you determine the brand you are creating. In example, when you prepare your meals every day, you typically walk in and out of places with that food. People will recognize that you hardly eat out and you always eat healthily. With this action alone, you can brand yourself as a healthy eater to everyone you see on a daily basis. If you also hit the gym at lunch every day, you will wear fitness clothes often. If you're eating healthy, going to the gym, and wearing tight fitness clothes, you will be looking fit, and it will show. That's an example of your brand. Be sure that your personal brand extends further than yourself by encouraging your clients live similarly to you, wearing your brand's products, and always having your business cards handy.

You can also think of personal branding as telling your fitness story and relating it back to your personal fitness theory. Communicate the trial and error you experienced as you put your physical training knowledge into practice and talk about how it led you to be in the best shape ever. You may have multiple stories that could be used depending on the clientele you wish to attract; keep in mind that athletes are different than weight-loss clients.

You can also think of personal branding as the clothes you wear, the things you do, and the lifestyle you live and how good you feel doing all of the above.

Lastly, create a name for what you do, and reference it when you are talking to potential clients or others so that they connect you with your brand. It can be as simple as using your own name or capitalizing on some aspect of your physique. It does not have to be elaborate or complicated—in fact, simpler is better.

Product Branding
Now that you have defined your personal brand, the next step is to turn that and your fitness theory into a tangible, sellable product, such as a twelve-week training program, a nutritional guide, a set of health tips, an exercise guide for specific areas, and so forth. It cannot be emphasized enough that you should know your target audience when considering product creation. Follow these steps to create a feel for your product:

- Define your audience: Decide who needs what your fitness theory offers. How old are they? Where do they live? What do they do?
- Define your brand: use your fitness theory to clearly define what it is you do.
- Create your brand name: Name your fitness theory. Simple is best.
- Tell your story: talk about how you came to create this amazing product or theory.
- Create a logo, tagline, and brand image: This usually entails hiring a graphic designer who can help with the color scheme and feel of your product. If you are promoting a natural brand, greens and other natural colors would be appropriate. For an athletic training brand, more aggressive colors such as red and black are appropriate. Expect to pay a good designer $200–$300 for a logo and branding colors.

Other types of branding can assist you with communicating your brand to your target audience:

- Cultural branding: discuss your company's intentions, work ethic, and integrity.
- Service branding: Explain how you deliver what you sell or do.
- Destination branding: Decide how people will feel after having worked with you and achieved results.

Business Checkpoints

Now that you have taken the time to get credentialed and master your craft, it is time to think about the business elements of starting your own personal-training business. In this section you will find a list of necessary things you must consider before starting your business.

Name Your Business
Before you get too sold on your business name, check its availability through all the facets of potential registration. Type your potential business name into the following websites to check whether anyone is using it for a business in a health- or fitness-related field:

- The United States Patent and Trademark Office is the federal government's inventory of trademarked business names. Unless the name you have chosen is for a completely separate industry, such as automotive, if your business shares common words or phrases and if they are considered live, then you must choose a different name for your business. From the USPTO.gov website, locate "Search Trademark Database" under "Learn about the Process," and then click the "Trademark Electronic Search System (TESS)."
- The secretary of state's office will let you know whether the name you are interested in using is currently registered in your state. Some people do not trademark their business names but do register them in the state they are in, so this is a necessary step to ensure your legal safety with name selection. The web address for this office varies by state, but it should be similar to SOS.CA.gov for California or SOS.LA.gov for Louisiana, for instance.
- The web address for your business name is one of the most important items to check. One place to check is GoDaddy.com. For example, if your business's name was

Top Game Fitness, you would want to check the availability of TopGameFitness.com. There are ways you can change a potential web address if the name you want is unavailable. However, it is best to get the exact name of your business so your potential clients can easily remember it.

- Lastly, search engines, such as Google and Yahoo, will tell you whether your business name or a similar name is being used. Some people do not register their businesses at all but do have websites, Facebook accounts, or a company that might be using your name or something similar. You would still be legally allowed to use your chosen business name if you found something similar via a Google search, but it might cause confusion at some point.

Acquire Insurance

Personal trainers' insurance can be purchased through a multitude of insurance providers, but most certification companies partner with particular insurance providers to give great rates great rates for their certificate holders. NASM, ACE, NSCA, ACSM, and NCSF have partnered with InsureYourClub.com and offer the recommended $1 million limited-liability personal-training insurance for as little as $172 per year. This type of policy offers you protection from clients who claim that your training, advice, or products resulted in their injuries or illnesses. In addition—and this is very important—before beginning any exercise program or other service, you should create your own waiver and release-of-liability documents for your clients to sign. These will further protect you from legal issues. A simple Internet search of the term "fitness waiver" can deliver documents that can be customized with your company's name and logo.

Business Structure

Once your business name is settled, the registration process can begin. This will not only establish your business as a recognized entity at the federal and state levels, but it will also protect what you have worked hard to create. Assuming that you are selling personal-training sessions and fitness or nutrition programs you have created, it is important to know what steps are necessary to prepare for any legal issues from clientele. Begin by choosing a business structure that suits your business intentions. The structure does not have to be permanent, as you can choose another as your business needs grow or fluctuate.

There are two recommended business-structure options:

- Sole proprietorship: This option is one in which the business entity is owned and run by one person, and there is no legal distinction between the owner and the business. Although this is the least expensive business structure to choose and does not require much business upkeep besides filing taxes, there is a potential drawback that must be considered. Since you and your business are considered to be the same entity, anyone suing your business is also suing you. In other words, not only could a lawsuit wipe out your business, it could potentially put your assets at risk as well.
- Limited liability corporation (LLC): An LLC is a business structure that combines the choice for taxation as a partnership—or sole proprietorship—with the limited liability of a corporation, thereby separating you from your business. If a client were to sue, he or she could only go after the business's assets, not you personally. An LLC is not much different from the sole proprietorship option, but it provides more options as regards taxation that can be used to your benefit. Creating an LLC is more

expensive and also includes an annual fee (which varies by state but may be as much as $800) but think of it as an extra insurance policy that guarantees the protection of your personal assets. If you own a house or have a family that relies on you for income, the LLC is the way to go.

Register Your Business
There are a few ways to go about registering your business. The most tedious and time consuming includes filling out paper work and creating a package to submit to your local, state, and federal government. An alternative—and one that is highly recommended by many entrepreneurs—is to use LegalZoom. By simply clicking "Get Started" on LegalZoom.com, you can begin the registration process in a matter of minutes. Someone from LegalZoom will also call to make sure you are informed of anything unique to your business that needs to be addressed. As of this writing, the price for a simple business registry is $149, but it can be upgraded to include beneficial items depending on your budget. Using LegalZoom to file your business paper work leaves time for you to focus on the creative aspects of your company.

Organize Your Banking
It is necessary to create a dedicated bank account to handle all of your business transactions. Mixing personal funds with business funds can get messy at tax time and makes it difficult to prove actual business income. If you have decided on the LLC business structure you must wait until it has been approved by the state and you have received your employer identification number (EIN). Having the EIN number allows you to create business-checking and credit-card accounts that are separate from your personal ones. As your business begins to develop credit, you will

have access to higher credit limits. In addition, it gives you access to business loans should your business evolve or expand and you need funds to open a training studio or gym. Enrolling in online banking simplifies tracking business expenses, ordering business checks, and so forth. Following the guidelines of your chosen bank can minimize any fees associated with opening your business bank account.

Organize Your Accounting
Accounting can be both expensive and a big hassle if you are not sure how to go about tracking your sales and expenses. QuickBooks (QuickBooks.com) is a great accounting tool, but it is expensive (more than $200), and there is also a yearly renewal fee. We use GnuCash (GNUCash.org) at Fitness Mentors and can highly recommend it as it is extremely simple, free, and does not have annoying pop-up ads. Other options include Wave Accounting (WaveApps.com), InDinero (InDinero.com), and Front Accounting (FrontAccounting.com). There are many YouTube videos available that can assist you with the everyday use of these various accounting software options.

Once you choose an accounting tool and become familiar with it, there are simple tips that can streamline the accounting process:

- Put a monthly (or weekly) accounting session into your calendar in which you log into your online bank account and record every business transaction for that time frame. Set aside time to do this regularly, but it does not have to be daily (unless that is your preference).
- Create a receipt book that has each receipt stapled onto the calendar day the expense was incurred, and include a short explanation describing the reason for the expense

(lunch with a client, for example). Save every receipt because any expenses are write-offs for your business at tax time. In addition, the IRS will need to see the receipts if you do get audited.

Understand Additional Considerations
Depending on how busy you are, use a free customer-relationship-management software such as BitTrix24 (BiTrix24.com). This can help you organize all contacts you receive into one system, streamlining the process for customer acquisition and ensuring you have done everything possible to sell them your products or services.

As soon as your website is established, change your e-mail address to yourname@yourwebsite.com. This is extremely professional and helps to promote your business.

Purchase a cell phone to use as your business line. Every time someone calls, you should answer the phone with, "Thank you for calling (your business name). This is (your name). How can I help you?" Or say something similar to create an image of ultimate professionalism.

Social Media
So far, you have established a fitness theory and a personal brand, and you've defined your audience. You have a fitness program or some products, and you are ready to take the next step—selling to and building up a clientele. Social-media sites such as Instagram, Twitter, Facebook, Snapchat, YouTube, and Periscope will soon become your best resources for connecting with potential clientele. Although these resources may not necessarily attract the type of people that want one-on-one personal training, social media can bring you a steady flow of revenue-generating

clients. Almost everything you do with clients in a one-on-one setting can be adapted to meet the needs of people you electronically communicate with, and this is where your premade nutritional and workout guides become crucial to your business.

General Overview

Your social-media accounts should consistently convey your fitness message and be clear representations of your fitness theory, personal brand, and fitness lifestyle, whether through pictures (Instagram), videos (YouTube), social messages (Facebook), or messages of 140 characters or less (Twitter). Potential clients should see your various social-media feeds and be motivated to contact you to find out how they can be part of your fitness program or how they can purchase a fitness product you are promoting. This section is meant to teach you how to grow your social-media following by using your own fitness theory.

Following these steps can enhance your likeability and help create a vision of your fitness theory, but keep in mind to not over-post in any one category. Your pictures, videos, or messages should address each of the following topics in a strategically random order:

- Motivational posts: Think of a picture of Einstein with a superhot bod, doing single-arm pull-ups, hanging off a cliff, flexing his biceps, or drinking a protein shake, with a quote discussing the fact that he failed out of school but is still considered to be one of the smartest people to have lived. Or just use a quote or meme that aligns with your fitness theory.
- Fitness or health tips: Pull a small piece of information out of your fitness theory, and place it in an organized

picture, video, or written message that can truly help someone.
- Being a real person: People want to know that you are a real person with daily happenings that they can relate to. Show them your lifestyle—pets, food choices, struggles, accomplishments, family members, throwback pictures, and so forth.
- Humor: Everybody needs a good laugh. Posting something truly humorous or having deep irony will leave people itching to press the follow button. These posts will get the most likes, but make sure you are selective and appropriately promoting to your chosen target market.
- Promoting your business: It is okay to promote yourself and your products. Offering free materials and discounts on your paid materials will remind people you are here to help.
- A hot picture of your body: There, I said it. You now have my permission to flaunt what you've got, as these images will leave people doing double takes. Whether the picture is of your body or a body you appreciate, throw in some eye candy to gain interest from your audience. For images of women, show legs, glutes, and abs. For images of men, include shoulders, arms, and abs.

Be sure to be as active as you can on any social-media portal. Like, comment, retweet, repost, and don't waste time; you're there for a reason. Your responsiveness to your clients' questions and comments ensure you can provide them great customer service, as you are always available to communicate with them.

Now, let's discuss some tips to grow your following using different social-media portals.

Instagram

Using hashtags (#) to target your customers is going to be of great importance. Please check out http://blog.hootsuite.com/how-to-use-hashtags/ for excellent dos and don'ts for using hashtags. For example, when posting a picture about motivation in health and fitness, hashtagging the popular #fitspo (fitness inspiration) will place your post in a group that people looking for inspiring posts will view. Also, you can use the hashtag to locate people in your target market. For instance, people who want to lose weight might use the hashtags #weightloss or #weightlossjourney. You can search these hashtags to comment and like peoples' photos and generate their interest in following you back.

There is an advantage to browsing Instagram for a location nearby. When you know your potential clients typically hang out at a specific location, you can search for locations nearby to comment and like the photos posted there. Also, search for and use the hashtag associated with your city or area of interest to find people near your location. This can be a great way to build relationships with clients nearby who are interested in personal training.

Building relationships with larger companies can be a great way to get noticed too. Tag them in your posts, and chances are they will notice you. Comment on their photo, or message them to suggest a mutual shout-out or cross promotion.

Discover more at http://www.tintup.com/blog/the-ultimate-guide-on-how-to-get-more-followers-on-instagram/.

Twitter

Tweet and retweet often, and retweet interesting posts from your idols or areas of client interest.

Discover more at http://mashable.com/guidebook/twitter/.

Facebook

Facebook allows you to create and join groups that can benefit your business. If you search for groups about weight loss or health, you can directly target your audience with posts to that group. Continue to stick to the topics listed above. You can also create a Facebook to allow people to follow your business.

Discover more at http://boostlikes.com/blog/2015/01/ultimate-guide-increasing-facebook-photo-likes.

YouTube

Creative videos are tough to make, so attempting to be a real and relatable person is your best bet. Linking all other social-media accounts to YouTube can help increase your subscribers.

Discover more at http://www.incomediary.com/21-ways-to-dominate-youtube-the-ultimate-guide.

Snap Chat

Snapchat is one of the newer forms of social media, but it is already a big contender, on a level with the likes of Instagram and Facebook. Using videos of ten seconds or less allows others to get to know you better. With this in mind, be sure to post on all other social-media outlets that you can be followed on Snap Chat at your account name.

Discover more at http://www.forbes.com/sites/jaysondemers/2014/08/04/your-guide-to-using-snapchat-for-marketing/.

Social media is a great way to get the word out about your business, and it is free. Be aware that some platforms allow you to market directly to your niche at an extra charge, which can be a great idea. Always do your research, and you can create a great platform for generating income and helping people outside the in-person training norm.

CHAPTER 2
Give Away Free Information

Now that we are prepared and have created the successful start-up business we envisioned, it's time to bring the focus to the sales process. All the following sections in this book are geared toward attracting, selling, and maintaining the clientele necessary for a sustainable fitness business.

Determine Your Niche

The word niche has several definitions—in this case, it means "a distinct segment of the market." Choosing a niche enhances your ability to target and capture the attention of a select portion of the market. According to Dalgic and Leeuw (1994), choosing a niche is "part of a positioning strategy, and may be used as a deliberate marketing strategy to create business opportunities for many emerging companies." Determining a niche within the fitness industry is like picking your favorite protein shake—you may like them all, but you probably have a go-to flavor. The same pertains to finding your particular niche—your skill sets will appeal to a particular niche market.

Let's name some common niches in fitness. You can be as specific or as general as you want when choosing your niche:

- males or females
- youth
- seniors
- special populations
- rehab and pain management
- general weight loss
- muscle gain
- sports performance: basketball, soccer, baseball, football, triathlon, tennis, hockey, archery, and so forth
- CrossFit
- Olympic lifting or power lifting
- fitness competitors every damn person

The questions table 1 can help you in deciding which niche market you should choose.

Personality	Location	Fitness Theory
• Who are you? • What are your fitness goals? • What population wants to achieve the same fitness goals? • What type of people do you enjoy being around? • What do you do for fun?	• Where do you live? • What type of target population is abundant nearby? • Is this population large enough to sustain your business? • Does this target population have the means to pay for your services? If not what system can you create to make it affordable for them?	• How do you want to help others? • How does your Fitness Theory work for the goals of your chosen population?

Table 1.

To give an example of determining a niche, when someone first starts working out and all he or she wants to do is master the art of muscle gain and enhance sports performance, he or she could recognize that muscle gain typically caters to a more male-dominated population. Therefore, advertising and marketing toward males ages sixteen to fifty who are looking to gain muscle and improve athletic performance is a good idea. This population is specific but very abundant. You can still be open to training all populations, but your social-media posts and informative documents would target the struggles of gaining muscle and performing at your best.

Now, use the questions in table 1 to describe the type of client you would have the most enjoyable experience with. This will be your chosen niche.

Target Your Niche

When it comes to targeting your niche, the type of information you give out needs to be directly tailored to your potential clients' needs and motivations. Use the ideas below to correctly identify the best way of doing so:

The first step in targeting your niche is to focus on the what. In being a part of or studying your niche, you should have an idea of what target audience's main fitness and health concerns are. For instance, writing tips on how to reduce postpartum baby weight is not going to appeal to an audience of senior citizens. Having some idea about the answers to the following questions can help connect those concerns and interests with the subject matter you want to promote:

- What does my niche do?
- What are my niche members' common barriers to exercise?
- What motivates my target audience?

- What does my niche want to improve?
- What type of magazines or online articles do my niche members read?
- What are my niche members sharing on social media?
- What TV shows do members of my target audience watch?

Where should be a simple question for you to answer, but be creative in your thought process. For instance, where are people most likely to be open to discussing their health? Creating a list of foods that help to improve fat metabolism and handing it out by a health-food store could lead to meeting people interested in improving their health. Table 2 is a comprehensive list of amazing places where you could focus your efforts, but be sure to choose places where your chosen niche would most likely go.

Public / General	Fitness/Health/Beauty-Related	Multi-media
Bridal / wedding boutiques	Fitness expos	Facebook
Business offices	Gyms	
Church	Hair / nail salons	Instagram
Coffee shops	Juice bars	
Parks / beach	Supplement stores	Twitter, etc.
Sporting events	Tanning salons	
	Yoga, Pilates, Spin classes	

Table 2.

It is also very helpful to build up a network—word of mouth can be key to establishing your clientele. Who do you know? Ask them to spread the word.

Personal	Professional	Alternative
Acquaintances	Chefs	Acupuncturists
Family	Chiropractors	Chinese medicine
Friends	Dentists	Herbalists
Moms (they work hard!)	Doctors	
	Nurses	
	Nutritionists	
	Physical therapists	
	Plastic surgeons	
	Talent agents	
	Wedding planners	

Table 3.

As for when to market, network, and target your niche, that depends on the habits of your potential clientele. You want to reach out to businesses during their normal business hours; juice bars and coffee shops will be busiest in the morning. Nail salons and wedding boutiques are busiest on weekends.

Create Opt-In Opportunities

When you opt in to a blog or newsletter or enter a contest online, the website collects contact information from you, which gives the owners an immediate link back to your inbox and allows them to reach out to you soon thereafter. The spam e-mails everyone receives on a daily basis are a result of companies or websites who have your information selling it to other companies, who send the spam, hoping their products are something you would be interested in buying. That said, as a personal trainer, your vigor to build your client base should be no different, except hopefully, you are building value in your attempted outreach. The purpose of collecting as many e-mail addresses or phone numbers as possible is to further client relationships by building trust with them and staying in their daily thoughts on health and fitness. But how do you collect and build upon your e-mail or contact lists and then capitalize on that information to build clientele?

Let's first take a look at what happens at fitness tradeshows. You show up at your nearest convention center psyched about all the free shirts, fitness tools, and supplements you are going to get. You visit every booth you possibly can, like eleven-year-olds on their first Halloweens without their parents slowing them down. You get enough preworkout and protein powder to last you a decade, and you're ecstatic. In the process of collecting all of this amazing swag, you probably have to do a few things to receive it. One of them is definitely signing up, or giving out your name and e-mail address. Or maybe some companies have you give them shout-outs on popular social-media outlets. But now, your childish greed has riddled you with e-mails from twenty different companies at least once a week. But you cannot deny that you are now more inclined to purchase their products. This is the point behind opt-in opportunities; create relationships, and encourage action until people buy. Let's take a moment to recognize ways we can build our e-mail or contact lists.

This chapter is called "Give Away Free Information," but when you think about it, it is not really free as people pay with their contact information. Here is a list of value-building ideas that are meant to entice your target market to give you their e-mail addresses or phone numbers.

- Written informational material: Informational articles are meant to directly cater to your niche's needs and are best delivered via online platforms. There are thousands of other ideas that you can come up with that will meet the needs of your niche, so be creative:
  - workout tips—"Five Great Outdoor Exercises"
  - nutrition tips—"Three Foods that Crush Belly Fat"

- seasonal health tips—"How to Lose Weight through the Holidays"
- body-part workout tips—"Four Booty-Blasting Exercises"
- general health tips—"Why Your Sleep Is Preventing Fat Loss"
- exercise facts—"Why HIIT Cardio Is Better than Steady State"
- promotional ideas—"Why the Jennifer Method Trumps CrossFit"
- In-person free services: These services work great for personal trainers, as you get to spend five to ten minutes proving your value with the potential client's direct attention. Be sure to have a clipboard present with sections for names, e-mail addresses, and phone numbers.
  - Body-fat assessment
  - postural assessment
  - cardio and respiratory testing
  - fifteen-minute ab workout
  - flexibility session
  - new fitness-equipment tutorial
- Tangible products: In-person opt-in opportunities are more productive when a physical object or service of perceived value is presented for "free" (costing only contact information). People will be lining up around the block to get something they perceive as valuable (remember the tradeshow reference):
  - inexpensive fitness equipment (stability balls, myofascial-release tools, measuring tapes, etc.)
  - health-food items or supplements you recommend
  - promotional towels, cups, pens, mugs, shirts, wristbands, and so forth
  - autographed seminude pictures of yourself (you know they want it)

I previously discussed customer-relationship-management software, but it is very important to use when selling things at a high price point like personal-training packages, so let's quickly revisit the basics. Now that you have all of these new e-mail addresses and other contact information for potential clients, they should be organized. Placing your contacts in this CRM form allows you to implement a protocol for outreach. When dealing with three potential customers, it might be easy to remember where you met them, what they do for a living, and when you followed up with them last. But trying to do this for more than eight to ten people could be challenging.

I'm sure you've realized by now that giving away free information is crucial to the sales process. You can look at it as a lead-generation system. It can also be looked at as an alternative to paid advertising, but it does require your time.

The only thing left to do is to create your materials and test the responsiveness of your contacts. You will find that some materials work great and others do not. Through some trial and error, you will soon become a master at creating free information and building value to target your niche.

Bonus Opt-In Strategies

Below are twelve more ways to connect with your niche and drive your opt-in lead generation.

1. Sign up for every online personal-trainer site (niche directories). Niche directories, as mentioned above, can be very valuable for personal trainers who are looking to get exposure online. To be included on these industry sites, you simply need to add your listing to their directories, and you'll benefit from the exposure that these popular sites provide.

It can be challenging to find the exact locations on these sites where you can add your contact information, but the listing portals can usually be found in the footer. For example, one of the most popular personal-trainer sites in which to get listed is IdeaFit.com (which you'll also notice from the example above came up second in a search for "personal trainer west palm beach").

On this site, there is a link in the footer that says "Get Listed."

Figure 1.

Other sites may have portals in their footers as well, and this is usually the most logical place to look for them (unless a site puts the portal front and center on its home page). Also, many of these sites, like IdeaFit.com, allow you to list your information within their directories for free, but there may be some paid options as well.

How to Find Personal-Trainer Listing Directories
The best way to find these niche personal-trainer directories is to simply search the words "personal trainer" and a city name in Google and see which ones are the most popular in your area. You'll want to get on those first.

You can also get some solid directory listings by dong a search for "personal-trainer directory listings." Here are a few popular ones to get you started:

- IdeaFit.com
- iPersonalTrainer.com

- TRXTraining.com
- FindMyFitnessTrainer.com
- YouTrainer.com
- Handstand

These sites tend to rank higher in the search engines than your ordinary personal-trainer website will, so it pays to get on as many of them as possible.

2. Use your local chamber of commerce to sell group fitness packages to business owners based on employee-productivity research. As a personal trainer, you know that if you don't work out, you usually feel like crap. Well, the good news for marketing yourself as a personal trainer is that there is some scientific research that backs the aforementioned unscientific statement, and you can use that to get in front of lots of potentially great clients.

The scientific information, which was even covered by an article in Forbes, goes something like this:

- Businesses are more profitable when workers are more productive.
- Employees that work out are more likely to be productive because they have greater energy levels as well as higher self-esteem. These healthy employees take fewer sick days, have lower rates of absenteeism, and cost companies less in health-care costs, all things that lead to money saved.
- Companies that encourage or offer employees fitness programs can benefit from increased productivity and lower costs, and ultimately, profitability.

This strategy practically sells itself if you know who to sell it to. Guess what? I'm going to tell you who to sell it to. (Hint: here's where your local chamber of commerce fits in).

A great place to sell the idea of group fitness packages for employees is at a place where business owners congregate. One of the first places that comes to mind is the local chamber of commerce (although you can approach any other organization that may have business owners).

I know what you're saying: "Aren't chambers the types of places where realtors and florists go to try and get business?" Well, yes, but you are smarter than that because you'll make business owners want to come to you rather than having to awkwardly try to shake a million hands to hunt down the decision-makers and tell them about your great employee productivity and business profitability idea.

Here's what you do to sell fitness to business owners (assuming you are a member of the organization you are going to approach):

- Contact your local chamber of commerce (do a Google search for your city's chamber of commerce) and visit the "About" or "Board of Directors" pages to track down the contact information for the president or executive director. You may even want to call the chamber's general contact number to see who the appropriate person to speak with might be.
- Tell the chamber that you want to host a workshop on how group fitness programs can increase company profitability.

Hell, let's make this easy for you. Here's a script you can use:

Hello Director Gluteus,
I'm a new chamber member, and I'd like to get more involved within the organization. I'd like to hold a workshop at the chamber's offices on the topic of how group

fitness programs can increase company profitability. This is a research-backed topic that shows how an investment in fitness programs for employees results in increased employee productivity and company profitability.

Please let me know whether this something that you think the members would be interested in attending, and I can provide more details.

Regards,

Personal Trainer Bob

Now that you've gone directly to the source and asked for his or her help organizing an event that benefits their members, you'll probably get a resounding yes to your request. Now you'll have to begin to put together your presentation you've built up so much.

Using studies (*A*, *B*, *C*, and *D*) that you will research in the future as reference points, create a PowerPoint presentation that hits the following points:

- uses science to show how fitness results in decreased absenteeism and increased productivity and profitability
- shows your recommendations for group fitness programs that meet your criteria for helping employees stay physically fit (for example, twice weekly sessions)
- shows that you have already created an amazing program that people can enroll their employees in today

Now, the chamber is useful because it will market your workshop for you. To give them a proper nudge, request that they send out the news about your amazing workshop to their entire e-mail list as well as to their social-media networks. Also, make sure you emphasize that the workshop is for business owners or decision-makers so those people show up. The e-mail will likely also attract general personal-training clients, and that is not a bad thing!

To take action a step further, try to get the chamber to mention in their marketing that space is limited and that the follow-up e-mail should say "only a few seats left," or something like that, to showcase demand for your workshop. Get a list of all the attendees before or after the workshop so you can follow up on your own and thank them for attending.

Chamber memberships cost around $500 per year (give or take), so if you get just one client, it is likely your membership will pay for itself.

3. Partner with local health-conscious businesses. In the chamber example above, we learned how to leverage the power of a much larger organization to help market your own services. You can do the same thing by partnering with other health-conscious businesses. By doing this, you will not only get the exposure that the business can provide due to its much larger network, but you will also get a statement about your credibility if a credible business mentions your services.

For example, in my neighborhood, a local coffee shop that attracts a lot of young, active people hosts donation-only yoga classes every weekend. Generally, about ten to fifteen people show up for the hour-long classes, generating the instructor about $10 per student multiplied by the two or three classes she gives each day. At $300 to $450 a day for only three hours of work, it's not a bad partnership.

Plus, the instructor gets to make relationships with people who may be interested in her services and may become regular clients.

What local businesses do you think would make for good partnerships in your community? Take some time to explore opportunities, and determine whether your services would also be a good fit for the businesses you'd like to approach.

4. Make charitable donations. They're good for two reasons—tax deductions and free exposure—and for the purposes

of this personal-training marketing idea, I will focus on the latter. (Click the previous link to vet potential charities for specific tax information.)

Charity is actually a bit of a diamond-in-the-rough marketing tip that I have used before, and it has landed me quite a few new clients. Here's how it works; it's pretty simple.

Do some research on upcoming charitable events in your area by using Google. After finding one that you particularly resonate with, contact the event director to let his or her know that you are interested in assisting them and to see whether you could donate some personal-training sessions as a prize.

If your proposal is agreeable, see whether you can get mentioned by name (or website or brand) during the event, as well as on the charity's website and in its marketing materials. I found that offering a free three-pack of sessions is a great way to get exposure; it gives you the opportunity to turn whoever wins that offer into a client, and it allows you to get a nice little tax write-off if you do it right.

5. Get a booth at a swap meet or flea market. A swap meet is a gathering where like-minded enthusiasts get together to exchange items of common interest. You can get a booth at a swap meet or fair—gyms often do this—and offer things like body-fat assessments or hold fitness-related contests. For example, hold a push-up contest and give the person that does the most push-ups (within one minute) one or two personal-training sessions.

Collect contact information for each participant, and then just call everyone and give out free sessions in hopes that some people will actually become paying clients. A booth at a swap meet might set you back a few bucks, but if you are able to land a few clients, it will easily pay for itself.

You can find local swap meets in much the same way you found charity events above, by Googling them. Type "swap meet near me" into Google, and check out some of the local events. Then inquire about getting booths.

6. Offer healthy shopping outings. As a trainer, you know that nutrition is, for most people, more important than working out. This is why offering to take your clients to the grocery store and educating them on what you recommend that they eat is a great way to provide more value as well as show them how much you care about their results.

Shopping outings work best if you take clients one at a time to their favorite grocery stores and show them how to eat right based on their budgets, likes, and fitness goals. The idea is not to criticize them if they go straight for the Twinkies but to educate them on how balance in their diets can really help them perform at their peaks.

As a bonus, or if you want to upsell an additional service, let clients know that you will create nutritionally balanced meal plans for them that they can easily follow and get results. Whether their goals are weight loss, weight gain, or muscle gain, your expertise will allow you to create something valuable that will keep clients wanting to come back for more of your advice.

7. Host competitions against clients, and get local sponsors involved. If you really want to make a splash and go after some big public-relations exposure, this idea is for you. Hold your very own "Biggest Loser" contest with your clients, and set a start date when you take weight measurements or, if you specialize in another area, gains in the chest or biceps.

Once you have your pool of contestants, start sounding the horn. Get local businesses involved (I recommend health-conscious businesses, but they're not mandatory) and ask them to provide gifts in exchange for exposure, as part of a grand prize (and runner-up prizes). From there, you'll also want to get the local media involved to see whether they will cover the story. The media loves this type of feel-good story, so if you can get them to agree to cover your contest, you'll benefit from a lot of free exposure (as will the local businesses that you involve).

After the contest is over, let your participants and the media know who the winner is. You'll want to take before and after pictures and promote them on your website, at your local gym, and on social media to show progress and how great your training is. You can also use the contest to continually market yourself and use clients' testimonials for social proof on your efforts.

8. Advertise that each existing client can bring a friend to any personal-training session, anytime, or advertise that you are opening up sessions to include the ability to bring in friends. This works well because friends like to work out with friends, and if you open up this promotion for free, your clients will actually feel good about giving the gift of health to their friends.

This practice works best if your clients tell you that they want to take you up on the promotion so that you can provide them with signed waivers with specific dates (you'll especially need to use signed waivers if you train at a corporate gym). The idea is to give your clients something tangible—the nicer looking the waiver is, the better—that they can hand to their friends.

When the friend comes in to work out with you and your client, it will be easy to get to know them quickly. When they see how badass you are and how great it is to share your fitness knowledge, they'll be more likely to sign up for their own sessions.

9. Offer package pricing to encourage long-term relationships. You may have heard the old marketing cliché that a new client costs five times as much to acquire than an existing one does to retain. Whether this is true or not, the reality is that more time should go into wowing your existing clients than into trying to drum up new business.

Think of cell-phone companies—does it piss you off that all their promotions are for new clients, and existing long-term clients get the shaft? The lesson here is not to be like cell-phone companies: benefit from existing clients by upselling them and keeping them around for the long haul.

One of the best ways to do this is to offer package pricing—something like buy five sessions, and get one free—to create real value for your clients. This not only extends your relationships, giving you more time to prove results, but it also shows your clients that you care about their wallets.

10. Buy a specific piece of equipment, and invite people to use it. Sometimes just by being seen, fitness equipment can promote your ideas better than you ever could. For example, I bought a slide board and invited people to use it at an ice-skating rink. Slide boards are particularly helpful for building strength and endurance in the legs, and my goal was to attract both hockey players who wanted a competitive advantage as well as figure skaters who wanted to improve their strides.

As people approach your special-equipment area, try to recruit them as clients, or put them on your marketing list by making them sign up to get involved. Give them free tries on the equipment, and explain the benefits of it, paying particular attention to their fitness goals. Just make sure that everyone who wants to try your equipment signs up for your marketing list so that you can reach out later.

Other cool equipment includes tractor tires, battle or climbing ropes, and so forth.

11. Do fitness competitions yourself. Enroll in a body-building competition, such as a figure competition, and the exposure you get from the competition as well as the social-media marketing you do to promote how good you look will help spur leads.

CrossFit trainers participate in events all the time. You'll often see trainers in CrossFit games or similar competitions sporting their gyms' attire, all the while doing wonders for their own exposure. Not only will people get to see you in action, putting your strength and training techniques into practice, but they will also see that you train at a gym, providing you instant credibility and attracting attention to your gym or brand.

12. Embrace the power of cross referring. Personal trainers are not isolated in their aims to help clients get healthy. There are lots of other health and fitness professionals that help people become their best selves in ways that may not necessarily involve weight training or exercise.

The following are the types of professionals you should seek out—start with five—so that you can cross refer clients to one another. Think of local nutritionists, chiropractors or physical therapists, physicians, hair stylists, massage therapists, sports coaches, and so forth whom your clients may benefit from. The referral partnership should be communicated and understood—don't just refer them clients without letting the other professional know that you'd like to try to consciously cross refer—and be proactive about your referrals.

When referring, go the extra mile, and call the professional with your client standing next to you, or shoot the other professional an e-mail, and cc your client so that the connection is actually generated. Don't just say, "Go visit Dr. Jones." Form the connection, and you will benefit from instances when your referral network does the same for you.

CHAPTER 3
Offer a Free Service

The goal of offering free information is to collect potential clients' contact information in order to help them along the sales process. By offering that free information, product, or assessment, you are able to make them aware of who you are, what you represent, and most importantly, what services you offer. When they are aware of your services, you still can't expect them to be ready to jump in and purchase. This is why a free taste of your full services is necessary. This chapter will discuss the necessary continued sales process that will bring customers closer to buying by continuing to build value as you offer them the full service experience for free.

Decide What Services Will Attract Your Niche

You probably have an idea of what your chosen niche members want, including their fitness goals and overall health concerns, so it is important to now offer a service that will further their interest in you and the services you're selling. Let's take a look at what could further entice your target market. The general go to is to give potential clients a free taste of your services, like a fitness assessment and introductory workout, but describing the services as something more intriguing can increase the likelihood of the client partaking. Below are alternative ideas of niche-specific services to get your creative juices flowing:

- seniors
    - pain-management assessment
    - general health assessment
    - postural assessment
- athletes
    - strength assessment
    - cardiorespiratory-endurance assessment
    - power-and-performance assessment
    - flexibility-and-injury-risk assessment
    - nutrition-for-performance assessment
- those interested in general weight loss
    - body-fat assessment
    - cardiovascular stress test for endurance
    - complete health-and-fitness assessment
    - nutrition-for-weight-loss assessment
- pregnant or postpartum women
    - core-strength assessment
    - general fitness assessment
- people who want to get shredded, including gaining or toning muscles
    - strength assessment
    - circumference measurements
    - body-composition assessment (lean weight versus fat weight)
    - nutrition-for-muscle-gain assessment

Trust your knowledge about your niche to offer the most appealing service. Your goal here is to get potential clients to take advantage of your willingness to offer your services for free. You can add incentives like limited-time offers to make the call to action a quicker process.

Create Your Atmosphere

It is just as important to put the professionalism and effort into your free-service outreach documents as it is to be professional and attentive in person. Remember, this is not the first time the potential client has seen you or your company, so you must do something to build the atmosphere around your brand or style. Who are you? What image do you present? What feeling does your service create These are key questions to consider when trying to build your atmosphere.

You can imagine a poorly put together e-mail without images or colors that just has a bunch of exclamation points and says, "Take advantage of your free training session!" It's barren, with no vibe or feeling. The customer immediately compares your outreach to that of their favorite brands and associates your brand with an image of low quality. This is why it is so important to invest in an e-mail outreach company, like Aweber, Constant Contact, or Mail Chimp. Not only do these services manage all of your contacts, but they allow you to add beautiful templates to your company's e-mails. Although this requires a little time and effort to build, the reception of such a well-made e-mail bodes well for your customers' perspectives of who you are as a brand or person. If you can show them that you take the time and put in the effort to create organized e-mails, you will build the atmosphere of someone that puts time and effort into your training or other services. If you care about a simple e-mail, you will definitely care about your customers. Remember to cater to your personal brand and logo using consistent colors, fonts, edginess, and other aspects of your personal brand.

When you offer a free service, clients see something of value that they must take advantage of. Although a nicely put together e-mail can be a great way to offer a free service, it is not the only way. A phone call that engages the client in a more upfront way can be a great alternative. Having a prepared script for such phone calls is very handy. Be sure to practice this script on family and friends before unveiling it in order to work out any kinks in advance, giving yourself the best chance to convert a phone call into a potential client. Creating your atmosphere is even more important during a phone call, as everything you say, the way you speak, and how confident you sound is immediately creating a picture of who you are in the customers' heads. Below is a sample script:

Hi, is this Jessica?
Hi, Jessica, my name is Eddie, the personal trainer you met (or you had the assessment with, you signed up for the free product with, you saw on the website, or who wrote article about the five secrets to building a booty), and I wanted to follow up with you to see how you are doing in your goal to lose weight (or gain muscle or get in shape).

That's great (or that's too bad or well you're in luck). (Poke around their response by asking questions about the person's current success or lack thereof and how he or she feels about it).

Well, just to let you know, I am offering a free comprehensive fitness assessment and workout (or other service) to assist you in your goal (be sure to be specific about the person's goal). I will be doing everything, including body-composition testing, postural analysis, and cardiorespiratory testing, to see what your current level of fitness is. This will allow us to see how we can grow and progress your results. Does this sound like something you'd be interested in?

(If the person says yes, move to this part of the conversation.) What days and times typically work best for you? (Sometimes, the person will want a further explanation of what will be taking place, so have an idea of everything you offer, and be prepared to describe it professionally.)

(If the person says no, say this.) Well, if you do know of anyone that you think would be interested, or if you would like to reconsider, please let me know as I only have a few time slots left. (Always make yourself sound booked when trying to sell; it will make people think everyone else is taking advantage of you and they are missing out.)

As a personal trainer, your success rate with the phone call would most likely be higher than with e-mail. This is due to the fact that people don't reject those they are speaking with as often as they will ignore an e-mail. The e-mail would be a great tool to use when selling a workout program or other mass-produced product. The atmosphere you create is always going to have a role in your sales process, and making sure that atmosphere aligns with what you want to project is crucial.

CHAPTER 4
Engage the Prospect

Focusing on a form of interaction with our prospective clients that goes beyond that of offering free information or free services is called engaging the prospect. We are looking to give prospects an idea of who we are and to give ourselves the opportunity to prove that we can help them. Why do we need engagement? To get people to buy! Most people don't buy things without talking to someone about them first, especially in fitness. The process of engagement can take place anywhere at any time, and it moves at a pace that makes both parties comfortable, sometimes quickly and sometimes extremely slowly. The pace is all based on whether the client recognizes the need for your services. To give an example, clients that research you online and are comfortable with how you train and your prices will be ready to talk about training with you the first time you ever speak; they might even ask you when you can start training them. On the opposite end of the spectrum, when you meet potential clients at public events and happen to mention you are a personal trainer, you can't expect them to have even considered personal training, and asking them whether they want to train would be overstepping the pace of the relationship. You can almost think about engagement as the courting process in a relationship; you can't ask someone whether they would like to be monogamous if it's your first date.

Hierarchy Of Engagement

In the hierarchy of engagement, we are looking to determine which type of contact is the most fitting for the current state of the client relationship. First, we must determine the different types of engagement, including face to face, via video chat or phone call, or using social media, text messaging, and e-mail.

- Face-to-face meetings: Highest in the hierarchy is the face-to-face engagement, and it is the main goal for each of the steps in the hierarchy, as it give you the best opportunity to either (a) confirming clients' already good impressions of you based on what they have learned from your website or materials you have created or (b) gives you the opportunity to make that good impression. Either way, as is the case for most industries, people are most likely to buy when they are in front of the salesperson. The goal of every other type of engagement is to make clients more comfortable accepting the face-to-face meeting.
- Video chats: Few people think of the video chat as a useful tool, but there some great benefits to using this type of engagement, especially for an online training business. Employing this type of engagement can give the client a sense of who you are based on looks, body language, confidence, and personality. This can build the trust of a client and move him or her closer to the sale. Using video also provides an opportunity to do assessments, such as posture or flexibility analyses, exercise forms, and some basic strength assessments, like push-ups and planks.

This media allows you as a trainer to prove your fitness competence and build more value into the service being provided.
- Phone calls: The phone is considered a middle ground in the hierarchy of engagement. Speaking with you without seeing you gives clients a sense of who you are and what your personality is like without truly giving them the whole picture. A ton of value can be built over the phone by asking questions to increase trust and understanding of one another, which can progress the client relationship. The goal of the phone call is to build up trust in order to move the client toward accepting a face-to-face interaction.
- Social-media posts: Although social media is a powerful tool, its hierarchy falls one step below the phone call because it doesn't allow for voice or face-to-face engagement. However, social media can be a first point of contact, and it is one of the best ways to meet potential clients and progress them through the hierarchy of engagement to closing the sale. Social-media posts should also drive your clients toward your up-to-date and professional website, thus maximizing their confidence in you, the trainer. And importantly, all social media should feature or link to an opt-in form for collecting e-mail addresses and other contact information.
- E-mails: E-mail might be one of the least effective forms of engaging the potential client, but due to the vast number of people that can be targeted with a single message, e-mail is beneficial. For instance, if you send an e-mail advertising your services to 200 contacts, roughly 70 percent, or 140 potential clients—will simply delete it without opening the message. Of the remaining 60 e-mail recipients, only 3 might click the link that takes them to

your website, and only 1 will reach out or respond. This is where the opt-in function comes into play. By funneling your social media outlets to your website where people will find a link to an opt-in form, a vast number of e-mail addresses can be collected. Increasing the number of e-mail recipients for your messages greatly improves the numbers of responses, or reach outs, you receive. Finally, every respondent has the potential for moving up to the top tier of the engagement hierarchy—the face-to-face meeting.

- Text messages: Texting really only makes sense if you have already converted a customer to a client. There are some reasons this form of engagement might be useful, such as when a client recommends a friend and gives you his or her phone number. Text messages are very non-threatening and allow the potential client to respond at his or her leisure. The goal of the text message would be to schedule a call or a face-to-face meeting, increase the potential client's trust, and close the sale.

Your First Impression

Regardless of the type of engagement, it is important to always bring your A game to the table when first contacting a client. You have exactly twenty seconds to make a good first impression (Brehm, 1-15 2004). If you have successfully engaged the client in that time, you can then begin the process of building further value. Below are some tips for building on the first impression and moving forward when engaging any client:

- Be prepared.
  - Know what your objective is for the given engagement. The goal of any engagement is to progress

potential clients toward sales, but sometimes further steps are needed. If an engagement is by phone, the intent could be to get the clients to agree to come in for a free fitness assessment. As such, be prepared. Practice your script beforehand, and try to anticipate any questions so you have ready answers.
- Know what your focus will be in progressing the current state of the client relationship. If your only contact has been via social media or e-mail, and you have progressed to a phone call—or better yet—a face-to-face engagement, your focus could be on getting to know the client in order to establish a more comfortable atmosphere moving forward. Sharing something about yourself (if the opportunity presents itself) can deepen the connection, as can projecting enthusiasm and passion for your chosen profession.
- Organize your tools beforehand. For instance, if you know you are doing a few assessments, be sure to have your paper work, tools, and space set up. This projects professionalism and attention to detail.
- Brand yourself.
  - Recognize that everything you do is a form of personal branding, including the way you look, what you wear, and even your personal hygiene. An in-person meeting or a video call gives you an opportunity to present the whole package.
  - Do not immediately deter a client by looking, dressing, or smelling as if you just finished a workout. Take your time to look professional. You should even go so far as to dress to what might make your client feel the most comfortable. For instance, when you have a client that wants to focus on muscle gain, wear clothing that reveals your physique to prove to the client

you have what he or she wants. With a client that is very overweight, wear fitness attire that is slightly looser to give the impression that you don't just care about looking fit. Below are more tips on physical appearance:
- Color coordinate your outfit.
- Wear your logo.
- Style your hair.
- Girls, do additional nice things, if that's your style (nails, makeup, etc.)
- Guys, shave (or don't, if that's your style).
- Wear some dope-ass shoes.

- Be attentive. Ask questions, and remember the answers. You are trying to progress the relationship. If you ask about a customer's family life, and he or she mentions two kids, ask more about them—names, ages, sports, hobbies, schools, and so forth. Then remember this information so you can ask the customer about it next time you see each other, regardless of whether he or she purchased training sessions.
- Be of service (regardless of the result). Remember that the outcome of the sale should not be your focus; rather, focus on what the potential client can learn and how they can grow. If they choose not to work with you, let them know that you are still available to answer any fitness- and health-related questions. Then, by continual engagement (via phone, e-mail, social media, etc.), the client can learn how he or she can attain fitness or health goals by joining forces with you.
- Be thankful. Thank the person for his or her time and for being gracious (rather than showing or projecting disappointment) to reinforce your professionalism. Even if a person doesn't work with you at this time, he or she

will remember how positive and caring you were, which can bring referrals in the future.

The Follow-Up

As we just discussed, the goal of engaging with a client is to build trust and encourage the sale of your products or services. If the engagement hierarchy has not yet led to a sale, it is important to reconnect while the meeting is still fresh on the client's mind. The follow-up is a chance to move the client up the hierarchy of engagement, and it will also give you another opportunity to close the sale. The follow-up process is typically done by phone or e-mail, and it occurs twenty-four to forty-eight hours after you have met with the client. Whether it is a phone call or an e-mail, the message must further solidify your professionalism and expertise.

Include the following information to properly create you go-to follow up:

- Express gratitude for the person's time and the meeting: "It was a pleasure meeting you yesterday! Thank you so much for taking the time to address your goals with me, as it really shows your commitment to improving your health."
- Encourage the person's goals: "Losing twenty pounds is something I think would make you super confident in your professional and personal lives, especially this summer when you're at the beach!"
- Explain that you are the answer to the person's goal (story and empathy): "I have assisted many clients in your exact situation, and a little time and effort has led to amazing results. I know it can be a challenging thought to trim down, but by combining forces, I think we can get you beach ready in no time."

- Refresh the person's memory about the time line for achieving the goal with you: "Since summer is only four months away, you can expect to lose about five pounds per month while training on average three times per week."
- Reference personal information the person mentioned to prove you are a great listener. Include their barriers to getting fit, and talk about what the person considers most important in his or her drive to achieve the goal (family, health, grandkids, career, recreation, fun, or sports performance): "Knowing how little time you have, we can make your goal achievable with specialized high-intensity interval training, which can get you in, out, and on your way to pick up Johnny and Sara from school."
- Close with a statement encouraging the sale: "Whenever you are ready to get started, I am here to assist you every step of the way."

Different client goals will create follow-ups that are different than this example, but hitting the main suggested points will prove your professionalism and encourage sales. Below is a sample e-mail addressing all of the above in letter form:

Hi, Derek!
It was a pleasure meeting you yesterday.

Thank you so much for taking the time to address your goals with me, as it really shows your commitment to improving your health. Losing twenty pounds is something that would make your confidence skyrocket in your professional and personal lives, especially this summer when you're at the beach.

I have assisted many clients in your exact situation, and a little time and effort has led to amazing results. I know it can be a challenging thought to trim down, but I think we would make a great team, and combining forces would get you beach ready in no time.

Since summer is creeping up, in three to four months, we can expect to lose that twenty pounds and the "spare tire" you mentioned. Typically, my clients lose about five to seven pounds per month while training three times per week, which is exactly what I would encourage.

Since you mentioned your lack of time being a difficult obstacle, we can make your goal achievable with specialized high-intensity interval training (HIIT), in which we will perform cardiovascular and strength-based circuits. This type of training can get you in, out, and on your way to pick up Johnny and Sara from school. I know they will be super excited when you're twenty pounds lighter and looking and feeling great as you run around with them effortlessly.

Whenever you are ready to get started, I am here to assist you every step of the way. If you have any questions in the meantime, please feel free to give me a call at 424-675-0476 or to e-mail me at Eddie@EddieLester.com.

Thanks again, and I hope you have a healthy and productive day.

Cheers!

Eddie Lester
424-675-0476
Eddie@EddieLester.com
EddieLester.com

When you master the sales process, most of these follow-up e-mails will be addressing the start of people's fitness programs and your excitement, but regardless, your follow-up is key to professionalism.

Continued Outreach

Staying in touch with your potential clients—whether with a monthly or weekly phone call or an e-mail—can be the thing that convinces a client who was previously on the fence to take the plunge and commit. In fact, staying in touch is just as important as reaching out to new potential clients. In either case, continued outreach will ensure your products and services remain in the minds of both new contacts and those you have engaged with in the hierarchy. Unlike the initial follow-up that addresses clients' specific fitness goals, continued outreach is meant to be more general in nature. Strategies can vary, but the object is to keep people interested in you and the services you offer. Continued outreach emails can be bundled with a free service or sent individually. Examples include the following:

- recipes and cooking tips
- new workout tools you are trained to use or reviews on how new tools work
- exercises for building better body parts (chests, backs, booties, shoulders, or tummies)
- client testimonials (with the client's permission)
- sales of your products or services
- promotional e-mails about your new certification or education
- tips and tricks to lose body fat, such as why too much cardio can be bad
- discussions of new research and how it can help people, or your reviews of the findings

Another potential way to create clients from your past engagements is to offer services or products beyond that of private training and promote these services in your weekly or monthly e-mails or by phone. One such service might use your skills in program design to create a workout program that clients can perform without you present that addresses basic fitness goals, like body-fat loss and muscle gain. The closing chapter of the book will address all forms of potential revenue generation, but understand that creating products that reach a broader market means more money for you and also helps more people.

At the end of all of your continued outreach e-mails, it is important to always remind your potential clients that you are their resource for success. Great statements can be "I am always here to help, and if you need anything, feel free to call me" or "I am just a phone call away should you have any questions about optimizing your health and fitness." Like the follow-up, continued outreach will ensure you keep your image as inviting and approachable as possible.

From understanding the hierarchy of engagement to making a good impression and from a great follow-up to your continued outreach, you must recognize that having a system in place that promotes optimal conversion of your leads is crucial. This system will take your business to the next level and create the financial freedom and great work-life balance that every personal trainer dreams of. Getting into the psychology of buying can prove to be just as important as the systematic approach of moving someone through the sales process.

CHAPTER 5
Prove You Care

What if you proved to a client that his or her health, happiness, and well-being was your number-one priority? Would that client be more likely to work with you? When analyzing all of the methods of sales, it is easy to focus on details about products and how they will benefit the users. But what if trainers could just genuinely listen to people and generate all the sales we need with little effort on our ends? Wouldn't it be awesome to drop that robot-like sales pitch and just let them do the talking? In this section, you will learn to understand the psychology of selling and how to place the selling emphasis on the customer.

Your Selling Personality

To some, selling may be seen as the exchange of goods or services for money. To others, it might be an exchange of goods or services that benefits both parties. However, when it comes to selling to different personalities, there is no straight line or perfect system. Defining the selling process can be just as difficult as the act of selling.

There are hundreds of selling strategies. Within the fitness industry, the product being sold helps determine the types of selling techniques that are used. The sales path you choose depends on your perceived ideals about what it is you are selling. Likewise, there are a variety of sales philosophies and personalities. Some example personalities are listed below:

- The instant friend: This person jumps into meeting his or her clients with an immediate vigor for a buddy-buddy connection. "Jerry! What's cracking? Those shoes are sweet! I'm doing a leg workout today, if you want to join." Being warm, inviting, and friendly goes a long way in sales and is a very common reason why people buy. The instant friend shows a genuine interest in what his or her clients say and listens intently to create an atmosphere of understanding. This approach can be very effective for the right type of clientele, but with the wrong person, it can be very off-putting and detrimental to sales. This type of person often dances on the friend-client border, which he or she must be careful not to cross.
- The guru: The guru is the sales personality you use when your knowledge is vast and no question a client has is a challenge. The guru has all the answers, and people must pay to receive them. This person's physique is stunning, and his or her attention to detail is impeccable. The approach is logical, and this person tends to stay away from conversations that might lead to connecting on an emotional level. This type of sales personality is really only possible once the guru has developed a track record, and the referrals and testimonials are abundant This person might discuss science-based articles and research studies, which can be dry but prove a high level of education. Type A analytical clients will be the guru's targets, as they recognize knowledge and respect it. The guru will deter talkers who need someone to vent to,

but don't worry; the guru wouldn't be able to put up with them anyway.
- The fitness consultant: The fitness consultant is a blend of the instant friend and the guru. Fitness consultants are eager to listen and connect, but they know when to step back and bring logical science into their selling. They can be considered experts with the clients' best interests at heart. The fitness consultant is extremely effective, and being one opens you up to many personality types, but it does require a lot of time, as you must weed through the emotional connecting to present the science behind your method.
- The network builder: Most trainers are aware of the importance of networking, but this person thrives in the social environment. Everyone knows that this person is a personal trainer and that he or she loves the profession. The network builder attends all social events with the intent to meet everyone in the room and engage each of them as potential clients. This person asks for referrals from all contacts and does well because of it. The better they are at network building, the more clients they will attain, regardless of what type of seller they are. However, the network builder effortlessly maintains contact with friends and acquaintances, thus creating a continuous client flow. However, they must be sure to back up their networking with client results and a solid educational base.
- The hard seller: This person has few cares except for completing the sale; he or she goes to the limits to get your business. This type of seller typically amasses the most clients simply because no is not an option. However, this person struggles to retain clients because the amount of effort expended on getting the sale dwindles once the actual training begins. Often, the hard seller will resort

to scare tactics or intimidation to gain the sale, which can create a negative energy around the person or the company that he or she represents. I don't want to deter you from using this method, as it is extremely effective, but back up your selling with effective training and client results. This type of selling can also be used as a last-ditch effort if your previous attempts were not successful (this is what big gyms might expect you to do).

Your personality may—or may not—fall into one or a few of these categories. The goal of using a personality is to create your own style of selling that aligns with who you are. Use trial and error to help develop what works best for you, and your sales success will increase.

What Product are you Selling?

In fitness, it is important to look at your products in a way that suits your selling style. When the old interview technique of "sell me this pen" comes up, the typical salesperson thinks he or she is selling a pen, plain and simple. The salesperson might say, "It has a great grip for your fingers and a smoothly rolling ball point for writing." The alternative thought that creates a good salesperson is not to think of describing the product but to focus on the result of what that product stands for. "This is not a pen; it is an idea. It is your next big idea that you will write down and use to change the world. Are you willing to invest in your own ideas?" Let's analyze a few ways to look at what a personal trainer is selling and how they can affect your chosen approach to sales:

- Your product is a twelve-pack of one-hour sessions lasting one month, with the fitness goal of losing ten pounds, and the package is priced at $900. With this method of thinking, you're creating a picture that your time as a personal trainer is valuable, so clients are, in a way, buying information within the boundaries of your time. A guru might use this technique, which creates the atmosphere that the end result is the knowledge the client will gain. This selling approach will probably be filled with explanations of the methods you use and how they are scientifically proven to give great results. It requires you to convince the client that you have the knowledge to be an effective trainer, which might mean a longer selling process.

- Your product is a body from a fitness magazine. You will definitely have clients that say they want to look like fitness models. With this thought in mind, you are selling the physical results of your training, which might happen in six to eighteen months. Your selling points are programming and maybe other clients' testimonials, putting the sales emphasis outside of the client. You might be looked at as a fitness consultant, as you probably care about the clients' results but also have the knowledge your clients want. This approach is great for the type of client that mainly cares about getting shredded. You are probably selling a bit more pseudoscience that has worked in the past but has no direct scientific links, so your past results will be your focus.
- Your product is the feelings of happiness and accomplishment your clients get from looking in the mirror and saying, "Wow!" Most trainers forget that almost all buying decisions are made based on an emotional connection to the purchase (Raghunathan and Huang 2009). Why not help your clients find this emotional connection to health and fitness, as they do with shoes or clothes? Everyone creates a story in his or her head

almost every minute of every day. Just as in the movie *Inception*, in which thoughts can be imbedded into one's mind, why not assist people to create a story that involve you and the emotions they feel when their hard work has paid off? The selling approach for this product includes digging a little deeper into one's personal emotions and asking questions about what clients truly want in life and why. This creates a connection that leads to a deeper understanding of the emotion behind a goal, connecting feelings with what you are offering. You might already be using this viewpoint if you consider yourself the instant friend, but it can be used by all personalities.

How you perceive the product being sold will guide the sales technique you employ. That coupled with your sales personality type will draw certain clients your way—and you toward particular client types. The goal of clarifying the product you are selling is to recognize which product to use for each client type. Drawing on the knowledge gained in this manual, your past sales attempts, and previous social experiences can assist you in this sales process.

Why People Buy

It is important to understand why people purchase other than what is needed for survival. What drives someone to buy a specific pair of running shoes or piece of exercise equipment? Most people who work for a living (and even those who are wealthy and don't have to work) need some kind of motivation to buy a product or service. According to Tauber (1972), "If needs other than those associated with particular products motivate people to purchase, the seller should incorporate this information into his marketing strategy." This section focuses on four areas that you must consider in your marketing strategy and when selling: (1) emotional connection, (2) credibility and trust, (3) perceived value, and (4) problem solving. Each section contains some personal experience I have encountered.

1. Emotional connection: As I mentioned above, almost all buying decisions are based on emotion (Raghunathan and Huang 2009). This means a buyer realizes that a product will potentially meet an emotional need. One goal for a seller of fitness packages is to allow a potential client to feel a sense of emotional connection toward the product or service.

Most personal trainers do not use the selling tool of creating an emotional connection to the product. They fill up time telling clients how they are going to get them to their goals. Have you ever heard of something selling itself? That is what happens when the emotional attachment occurs. Employing this technique can lead to your product practically selling itself.

According to a study done by Robinette et al. in 2000, implementing a strategy to connect with a consumer's emotion is based on equity, the experience, and energy. The following questions worked best to determine whether an emotional connection could be successfully created with a consumer:

- Equity: Does the trainer have your best interests at heart? Does the trainer share your values? Would you feel comfortable recommending the trainer to friends? What is your level of trust?
- Experience: Is the buying environment engaging? Is the trainer attentive and helpful? Is it pleasant to interact with the trainer?
- Energy: Is the process easy? Is the location convenient? Does the trainer respect and value your time?

Furthermore, attaching a positive emotion directly to your product can reap similar success. The goal with attaching a positive emotion to your product is to get clients to understand that they are in front of you for a reason, a reason they probably haven't even discovered yet. To give a brief example, a male client around the age of thirty comes to you and says he wants to get in shape. As a fitness professional, you recognize that this is not his entire goal. After speaking to him briefly, you hear him mention he wants to drop twenty pounds and gain back the muscle that he has lost in the last five years. When asked why he let himself slip, the client relates that his girlfriend, to whom he had proposed, left him a few months ago. You ask a couple of follow-up questions that allow him to relive the breakup slightly and create an emotional upwelling. This helps him realize he is ready to move back into the dating scene and take the next step toward getting back into shape. Once that connection is made, you are then able to ask him how comfortable he feels about himself physically, and he can admit his confidence is low, which makes him feel down. However, speaking with you makes him confident about the future, knowing that he will have a positive outcome after training with you, and he is ready to put in the time and effort needed.

    From a logical perspective as a trainer, you think: "You are out of shape. You are not happy being out of shape. You want to get back into shape. You need help. I am that help. If you get in shape, you will be happy. Training with me equals happiness. You are buying happiness. Therefore, I am selling happiness." With this thought process, your sales pitch becomes focused on a feeling the client will have when he is training with you to reach his goal, not on the physical goal itself. His new goal is happiness. Don't sell fitness packages to clients; sell self-confidence and happiness, but find new routes in your communication to get people to this thought. Once an emotional connection is made, the fee becomes a secondary issue, and the purchase is only a matter of setting the clients start date.

Not every story happens like this, and finding that emotional trigger is not always possible. Just remember that since most buying decisions are made emotionally, it is in your best interest to move clients toward connecting with that trigger.

2. Credibility and trust: From the consumer's perspective when purchasing fitness services, credibility is probably the highest priority. Very few people will purchase something of value without doing research into who they are buying from and what others thought of the product or experience. From personal trainers' viewpoints, credibility and trust come from sheer confidence in their fitness approaches or from referrals and testimonials given by current or past clients.

Confidence in your sales and fitness services comes from education and experience. You can imagine going to a doctor who has ten placards on the wall displaying his outstanding achievements in education—that makes you, as a patient, confident that the doctor you are seeing knows what is best for you. Although not all fitness clients look at credentials when purchasing training, your education can create trust and credibility for those you are selling to. If you are a trainer with more than six certifications, you can definitely impress people and build credibility just by mentioning them or having them listed on your business cards. At the same time, although you may have picked up some great tools from these extra credentials, most of your confidence comes from your experience working with clients and helping them achieve their goals. This confidence in yourself and the product you are selling goes extremely far when building trust with potential clients.

Testimonials also builds credibility and trust between you and your potential clients. Whether it be in a story you tell or pictures you show, a great testimonial allows clients to recognize that same needs as theirs have been met for previous clients you have trained. For this reason, it is extremely important to ask all your clients to write testimonials or reviews of their experience with you. If possible, include before and after photos, as a picture is worth a thousand words. With permission, be sure to photograph clients in formfitting clothing when they first start training with you, at the halfway point, and once they have achieved their goals.

Here are more ideas to help build credibility and trust:

- Sell a system: No one knows that high intensity circuit training using traditional and Olympic lifts for time gets people in shape, but everyone knows that CrossFit gets people shredded! If you have not developed your own system for getting people in shape (your fitness theory), research a fitness approach or system you closely align with and use it in your pitch for selling your fitness services. As an example, you can create your own system by explaining your daily training protocol: "Starting with self-myofascial release to address muscles that may be tight or causing pain, we will address mobility and flexibility to ensure you are moving correctly. Next, with a focus on functionality, we strengthen the most important muscles to support posture and proper movement. Once we are warmed up and moving well, we will then get into resistance training, with short rest periods to enhance the fat loss and muscle gain goals you mentioned." People see systems as somewhat guaranteed to work, because how else did they become systems? Similar to CrossFit, you can also brand your system, as labels further enhance credibility. "Muscle confusion" from the P90X series is one of the most popular catch phrases in fitness history.

Other examples include the terms "functional training," "postural enhancement training," and "myofascial compression therapy."
- Set up a time line: People like to be assured their goals are attainable within certain time lines. As a fitness professional, you are able to let clients know with confidence that if they stick with you and your training regimen, their goals are achievable within particular time frames. For instance, you could say, "In order to achieve your goal of being bikini (or cruise-ship or vacation) ready, we should train for three sessions per week over a period of four months."
- Communicate that the perceived value is higher than the cost: "It was such a good deal I had to buy it!" From a private-personal-training viewpoint, I do not recommend this approach. It's like shouting out, "I am the cheapest trainer in town!" Someone who is looking for a good personal trainer is not typically looking for the best deal. If you are just starting out as a personal trainer and want to gain experience, it makes sense to set your prices low, but as the traditional thinking goes, the cheaper the price is, the worse the product or service is. It is important to be realistic about what the market will support, but don't sell yourself short. Be sure that as your reputation for producing results grows and is backed up by testimonials, your prices also increase with each new client.

There are some cases, however, where you may want to offer a lower price, like building up a boot-camp or group-personal-training business. Group training gyms across the United States have used this method with major success. Certain niches such as youth sports or athletic teams can be targeted with this type of technique as well.

- Buying this product will solve a problem: Consumers make purchases because they need to find something they believe will help them fix issues they are having. As a fitness professional, you will encounter clients for whom pain is a daily companion. These clients will see your expertise as a hoped-for way of lessening or eliminating their pain. Using your expertise in observation and assessment to walk clients through their injuries, you can offer a program that will have them pain free—or nearly so. The goal of this type of sale is proving to people in this situation that *you* are the solution to their problems. We will delve deeper into this type of sale in the next chapter.

What Does the Client Want or Need?

The simplest form of sales is to address the needs of the client. Most people see this and say, "I do that all the time. Clients tell me they want to lose weight, so I show them how we're going to do that." *No!* Do not just tell them you will create a program that fits their wants and needs. I want you to specifically sell to their wants and needs.

You probably have a personal-training sales pitch, and if you don't, you will have one soon. Please throw that pitch in the trash. As soon as you get into a pitch about how your product or service is great, you shovel the first scoop out of your shallow sales grave. You lose the client's interest. "But my sales pitch works; I have gotten clients to buy!" Yes, your sales pitch might work for the select few who have already decided to buy, but why isolate yourself to a generic approach? Think of selling the pen again. Your sales pitch is, "This pen is soft and has a clip so you can attach it to your pocket." In other words, your description of the pen is a one-size-fits-all approach. Imagine as opposed to telling the customer about the details of the pen, you ask a simple question: "What would you do with this pen?" or "Why do you write?" The answer will give you insight into why the person is *interested* in buying a pen. When you know why he or she is interested in the pen, it will guide your individualized sales approach. With this versatile approach, you can create conversations that lead to greater understanding of your clients, and building sales will become a fun and easy process.

Below is an example of a dialogue that builds the sale with a potential personal-training client. The goal here is to show you how getting to know a person's wants and needs creates an easy environment to build the sale. Why does she need training, and what is she hoping to gain from it? A lot of small talk happens in between major questions, but the small talk have been left out to give you the main gist of the needs analysis. Notes are present to help you recognize the thought process that brings me to my next question or comment.

You've greeted the client with small talk about his or her drive over or sweet shoes. The client has signed the waiver and release of liability, and you've taken down basic general information:

> TRAINER. So, what is your biggest fitness goal right now?
> CLIENT. Well, I am really focused on losing about thirty pounds.
> TRAINER. When did you last feel as if you were in great shape?
> CLIENT. About four years ago. *Note: Four years ago, she was happy with where she was at.*
> TRAINER. What has changed in the last four years that has led to where you are now?
> CLIENT. I was working out more often, as I was a stay-at-home mom for my two kids. *Notes: I make small talk about*

the kids, their ages, and the local schools they attend. If her kids are the most important thing in her life, I will include their involvement in her goals, which aids my sales process. I also want to know why she is no longer a stay-at-home mom; it could lead to an emotional trigger.

TRAINER. Are you working now? *Note: This is an easy way of asking why she is no longer a stay-at-home mom.*

CLIENT. Yes. When my husband and I got divorced, I had to restart my consulting business, which takes up most of my time. *Notes: I make a bunch of small talk about her consulting business. This might help me determine her financial status and a potential schedule for our future sessions. She is divorced with two kids. I need to determine whether she is still upset about the divorce or has moved forward. This allows me to understand her emotional state further.*

TRAINER. So, your work and schedule has made it tough to find time for exercise.

CLIENT. Yes, that's why I have added the weight for sure. It's been a tough transition, but I recently saw a picture of myself that made me realize I need to make my health a priority. *Notes: Time is a problem and a potential barrier to exercise. Her divorce was troubling, but she is feeling better now. It appears she is serious about getting back into shape and wants to make health a priority (this is a huge selling point!). This will be the focus of my customized pitch. If she is truly ready to make her health a priority, we can start tomorrow. Also, her old self looked good—I must create emotional attachment to how she felt when she looked good.*

TRAINER. Would you say that you were in the best shape of your life at that point?

CLIENT. Yes. I wasn't very active growing up, but at that time, I was doing Pilates and yoga four times a week, so I loved the way I looked. *Notes: I make small talk about Pilates*

and yoga. *I use a small selling pitch about how I use those methods of training to build core strength, which is selling directly to something she attributes to looking great (I'm selling to the customer's wants and needs). She loved the way she looked at that point in her life.*
TRAINER. So, if we got you back to that look in four to six months, how would you feel? *Notes: There are many ways to ask this question, but the goal is to allow her to create an emotional connection between how she felt then and how she will feel during and after training with me.*
CLIENT. I would be so happy to have that body back. It feels so far away though. *Note: She lacks confidence in her ability to achieve her goal; I must sell her confidence.*
TRAINER. I actually just finished working with a client who was looking to drop thirty pounds of leftover baby weight, and with a little bit of sacrifice, we were able to get her there in five months. I know it may be tough to imagine now, but when you're back in that body in a similar time line, I know you'll feel amazing. Would that be something you'd be willing to work for? *Notes: There's a lot going on here. I told a quick story to build credibility and empathize with her; then I said a confidence-building statement to encourage the emotional attachment. I finished with a question asking her to take action on her emotion. She told me she wants to make her health a priority. If she is truly ready, she will say yes, allowing me to schedule her first session. The answer to this final question can go many ways, so be ready for anything. If she is not ready to commit, you'll need to build more value and create a deeper emotional attachment. If that doesn't work, you must attempt another sales method or resort to a hard sell. These closing techniques be discussed in the next chapter.*

Your new type of sales pitch becomes adaptable when you apply individualized selling. Remember you are selling to your clients' needs, which means you must find out what they want and tell them that is what you offer. If a client says, "I want tacos," you'll say, "You came to the right person, because I am selling tacos." Or to be more literal, if a client says, "I want self-confidence, and I love suspension training," you can say, "My specialty is TRX, and that can really help you build your self-confidence." To put your sales into a new perspective, you are no longer the trainer that offers *XYZ*, you are the trainer that finds out what your potential clients want, and you present it to them in individualized packages.

Power Questions

Getting to know your clients is an important aspect in any sales environment. Asking the right questions allows you to discover needs, values, and morals so that you can design sales pitches that will align with each trait. Power questions are designed to not only to expand the discovery of client information but also to guide the client to a specific answer. Ideally, that answer will coincide with the realization that they need your training or services. There are two categories of power questions—directive (closed ended) and nondirective (open ended):

- Directive questions: Directive questions are asked to guide the client toward an answer and are typically designed to connect the client to the system or services you are offering. For example, a directive question is "if you knew that training with me would pay off three months down the road, would you start today?" This line of questioning leads to either a yes, a no, or a maybe. If the answer is yes, then a sale may ensue. If the answer is no or maybe, then further questioning is needed in order to discover what sales barriers may exist. You can also use directive questions to reinforce a statement such as, "You mentioned your goal is to get back in the shape you were in four years ago." And perhaps reinforce that with, "You mentioned your goal is to gain back that self-confidence you felt from being in great shape." These questions can be used to discover a client's motivation for buying, which in this case is to gain back self-confidence. Remember that people are more willing to buy an emotion like confidence, which can be the driving force of a successful sale.

Listed below are more questions that I recommend adding to the general questionnaire you use when interviewing and selling to a new client. I have also included a summary on how or why to use them:

- Can you commit to achieving your goal? This type of question provides an outlet to see how serious your new clients are about actually putting in the work to achieve their goals. If they are serious, this is an easy question to answer. If they beat around the bush, you can identify where they feel like they need help or possible barriers to fully committing.
- What are the top three priorities in your life currently? This question may seem as if it is open ended and requires an explanation, but it is actually quite directive. You are asking clients to point out three things that they live for. People will typically answer family, career, and friends or fun, or a variation of those three. How they answer this question opens a door to a useful sales technique. Since they typically don't consider their own health as one of their top

three priorities, which is probably why they are out of shape, ask them, "How do you feel improving your health would affect those three priorities?" This directive question helps people understand that committing to getting in shape improves their lives so they can better enjoy the things they care about most. If they do include health as one of the top three priorities, it will be easier to sell them, as they already know they should focus on their own health and that *you* are the person to help them do that. The hard-sell version of this question is, "Do you want to be able to keep up with your kids as they age?"

- Why did you decide to meet with a trainer (or with me)? The answer to this question may be obvious, but it reinstates that clients are meeting with you because *you* are the one that can help them achieve their goals. It can also be a good gauge for establishing how they feel about you, or about personal trainers in general. If they have not had good results using trainers before, they may be doubtful about achieving their goals with you.

- What three things do you want to buy right now? This question will allow you to compare clients' other buying interests with your service. If you know what else is in competition for your clients' dollars, you can relate and better encourage the use of your service. Further questioning along these lines can bring clients to the conclusion that achieving their fitness goals and feeling healthy are just as—or more—important that any materialistic purchase. Using this as a hard-selling technique, you will have the chance to prove to them that your service is their number-one priority.

- Nondirective questions: Nondirective questions give clients opportunities to share information about themselves. This allows the personal trainer to gain much-needed information about who clients are and how to sell to them. Questions such as, "What was your experience like working out in the past?" allow your clients to express what they enjoyed or disliked about working out, which can give you insight into how to pitch the product or service being sold. These types of questions can also be great for instigating a client's own self-discovery. For instance, questions such as, "Where does your motivation for this goal stem from?" entice clients to think about exactly what has brought them to the tipping point of seeking out your services. Getting deeper level of understanding about clients' motivations can give you selling points to focus on.

  Add these power questions to your general questionnaire to get your clients to open up and allow for deeper understanding of how to sell to them:
  - How do you feel about your current state of fitness and health?
  - When you stand in front of a mirror, are you happy with the way you look?

    (These first two questions can be used interchangeably in an attempt to connect an emotion to the client's current physical state. Most likely, clients will not feel great about themselves, and you can assure them that with you, that feeling can be changed or that by working with you, not only will their physical states change but so will their mental states, as their feelings of self-worth and confidence improve.)
  - How important is your health to you? Many people's own health sometimes takes a back seat to other

things in their lives. This question allows clients to freely discuss the importance of health in theirs or their families' lives. Whether they answer that their health is very important or that it is not a priority, you can tailor your sales technique and pitch to either scenario.

- What other things have you tried to get into shape? You are trying to target any experience that a client liked or disliked. When you know what they like or dislike you can tailor your pitches to ensure they are in line with your potential clients' most enjoyed methods of fitness and health.

- What is currently keeping you from achieving your goal? Acknowledging barriers can be a great way to prove that you care about every aspect of a client's journey to getting into shape. Verbalizing or communicating the causes of these barriers allows you to address ways of dealing with them—possibly by working around a challenging schedule, family obligations, or other issues—and you can pitch your service to avoid conflict with those barriers: "I can schedule a workout routine that fits within your time limitations."

- What do you like to do for fun? Finding a common ground of things that you both enjoy can develop an easy connection and stimulate great conversation. If you both like surfing or hang gliding, a sales pitch might be geared toward strengthening the muscle groups needed for those sports. If you don't share the same interests, do some research to be knowledgeable about the things your clients enjoy most.

- Why, why, why? It is important to use the why questions when you are looking to delve deeper into a client's fitness goal. If a client comes to you and says,

"I want to lose forty pounds," it is imperative to understand why. There is a big motivational difference for a client who answers, "Because I want be healthy for my family," versus someone who says, "Because I don't want to die young, as my father did." The more you understand why, the more you will be able to tailor a sale toward that individual's motivation.

Proving that you care about your clients and their best interests is one of the best ways to develop sales. Why would you want to spend time training with someone that doesn't know who you are as a person or what your goals are (training or otherwise) or who doesn't care about helping you? This should not be a challenging task (although some clients may be more difficult to get to know than others), but as a trainer, you should be genuinely interested and concerned with your clients' journeys to achieve their goals. The client-trainer relationship should always be professional, but many business relationships pivot on the friendship qualities of trust and understanding. Striking that balance is imperative.

CHAPTER 6
Close the Sale

Setting Your Prices 📄

Before discussing pricing with any client, it is imperative that you are confident about your current rates. So, let's look at how you can set prices to align with the current state of your business.

From a mental standpoint, all sales begin with setting the right price. Unlike working in a commercial gym, private personal trainers have the option to set their own prices. Below are a few factors that will affect your pricing:

- Location: Where in the world are you training? Location is a top priority when setting your prices. You can think of two trainers located in Los Angeles, California. One of them is located in Beverly Hills, and the other is located in Compton. In Beverly Hills, one hundred dollars per session would be completely reasonable, while the same price in the city of Compton would be laughed at. This is due to socioeconomic conditions within the individual suburbs. Be sure to align your pricing within the attainable range of your community's target population, or commute to a different location to train.

- Economic conditions: What are your prices? In an economic downturn, one of the first things to be cut from a client's budget is personal grooming. Nail, hair, massage, and personal training appointments will all be gone. It is important to be aware of the economy in order to adjust your prices accordingly should a recession occur. People will be more likely to train with you if you show understanding of the current economic conditions.
- Personal branding and image: How are you attempting to brand yourself? Are you the organized trainer with the newest in-style clothing, who is driving a BMW? If you are, you can set your prices to reflect your elite professionalism. Remember that people sometimes associate a premium price with a premium product and a cheap price with a low-quality product.
- Target population: What is your target audience? You have a fitness theory, you've developed materials for outreach, and you know your potential audience. It is important to understand your niche and to market to those people specifically. Setting prices that are attainable by your target population absolutely determines your sales.
- Cost to train client: How much are you spending to complete your service?
  - Travel time to client: A client who lives twenty minutes away versus one who lives five minutes away can be reasonably expected to be 30–50 percent more per session (unless they are willing to head your way).
  - Gym payment: As a private trainer, having to pay a gym fee for training at an established gym is very common. Anywhere from ten to twenty-five dollars is normal and thus must be added to your total session price.

- New tools: What new equipment have you invested in that will benefit your clients' experiences? Training in a park with some bands and a stability ball is less valuable than having access to a full gym setup, including barbells, weight plates, dumbbells, kettlebells, a TRX, and a prowler.
- Self-worth: How much do you believe your time is worth? When determining your pricing, it is important to recognize that self-worth matters more than all other factors. You can set your per-session rate at any price you want, but the question you have to ask yourself is, "Do I believe someone would pay me that much for my services?" Your worth is determined by the following factors:
  - Experience: How long have you been getting people to their goals?
  - Education: Do you have a CPT certification (or more than one)? Do you have a bachelor's or a master's degree? The more education you have, the more confidence you will gain, and therefore, the more you can charge.
  - Personal beliefs: What do you believe you are worth? I have asked this question to many new trainers and gotten a variety of answers. Many new trainers have told me that they would work for free to gain experience before they would charge. Others have told me they are worth twenty dollars per session. I have also had brand-new trainers confidently tell me they are worth sixty dollars per hour. All of these trainers were able to get clients at those prices because they were confidently charging exactly how much they believed they were worth. Sometimes, even setting a

price that is five dollars too high can break your confidence. When you are looking to set your own prices, it is imperative that you ask yourself your worth with truth and honesty. When you ask yourself what you are worth, make sure that beyond a shadow of doubt, you are not oversetting your prices, because if you do, it will hinder your ability to sell.

Early in my training experience, I was recently certified and charging friends and family twenty-five dollars per hour to train with me. I applied for a position at the nicest gym in town and got the job. I was excited to get started and find a ton of clients. Unfortunately, I was going through new-client consultations over and over with little success, and I realized when it came to discuss the pricing to these potential clients, I had very little confidence. I was trying to have people pay eight-five dollars per session when my self-worth was only at twenty-five dollars per session. I was doing a great job building value and telling people all about how much they would benefit from working with me, but they could see the lack of confidence when I was discussing the prices. Subconsciously, I was telling them, "I am not worth eighty-five dollars per session," and they were confirming that by not buying.

It took me two months to get my first client. My worth was not aligned with eighty-five dollars per hour, but my manager assisted me by closing my first sale for me. After training this client for two to four weeks and seeing his progress and results, my self-worth grew. The experience of getting someone true results allowed me to go into my next sales attempts with the confidence to say, "I am worth eighty-five dollars per session because I will get you great results" with zero doubt in my voice. People agreed, and my clientele began to expand.

How do you increase your self-worth? The best thing you can do is put time into gaining experience and expanding your education. Do workshops, get more certifications, and train more people. Do whatever you can to be able to confidently discuss your worth at a higher rate. It may take a few months or maybe even a year, but once you see your clients with new outlooks on their health, you will realize how much value you truly have.

What if your gym requires you to charge a rate above your self-worth? Find your confidence for charging that amount in the brand name of your gym. Attempt to detach yourself from the current state of your training, education, and experience and know that your company is confident in those rates and is confident in you, as it hired you for a reason.

Discussing Pricing

"So, how much do you charge?" Nothing is more important than confidence when discussing pricing, and part of that confidence comes from knowing you are charging what you believe you are worth. But let's look at different ways you can unveil the pricing of your services. Remember different selling personalities will choose different routes to discussing pricing, so refer to the selling personalities section of the previous chapter if needed.

You will typically see brochure pricing in commercial gyms. They will have premade brochures with lists of prices, typically lowering the per-session cost when a client purchases more sessions. When neatly designed, a brochure can show professionalism, and they allow clients to feel secure in the knowledge that they are getting consistent prices. It is important to properly explain the price per session as well as indicating more sessions mean a better deal. As a private trainer, you can choose to have brochures; just remember to incorporate that extra cost of making the brochures into your per-session rate.

Open prices are delivered verbally and sum up the clients' goals and time lines to achieve the goals. This type of pricing also takes into consideration the location of training, the number of sessions per week, and the potential gym fees you will be required to pay. With this pricing structure, you can offer a few different options for the client to choose from. For example, you can say, "If you want me to travel to your house to train, each session will cost eighty dollars due to the extra time it will take me to get there. If you want to train in my home-based gym, the cost will be only sixty-five dollars per session. If you would like to train in a gym near your house, the cost will be eighty-dollars plus the gym fee of fifteen dollars, totaling ninety-five dollars per session."

When using an open pricing structure, your ability to gauge clients' financial statuses can affect pricing as well. If a client is a lawyer and lives in an expensive neighborhood and drives an $80,000 car, don't be afraid to add $10–$20 to the per-session price. If you are desperate for clients, you can lower your price by $5–$10 for someone who you know has a lower financial status. This style of pricing may even be negotiable so that you come to the sale with both parties feeling content.

Having a single price means you do not need a brochure, as it is a firm, set-in-stone number. A single price can suit an expensive trainer's style and requires great confidence. You may recall how to include the client's emotional connection when discussing the price. For example, you could say, "To get you feeling confident in your own figure when your family comes to town this summer, we need to train three times per week for four months. I charge one hundred dollars per session, which can be paid weekly, biweekly, or monthly." This type of pricing should be used when optimal confidence is achieved and your schedule is already relatively full.

Picking a Pricing Structure

The goal of all your hard work to be a certified fitness trainer is to make a living as one. You have gotten the certifications, validated your fitness theory, created outreach materials, rehearsed your sales pitch, and confidently begun building up your client base. Your communication skills are enhanced by more experience, and you know the worth of your products and services. How do you set—and get—your price? I will now give examples of two pricing structures that can be modified to suit your selling style and budget goals. The first is a pricing structure that might be suitable if your client is new to you and is not convinced that he or she is ready to commit yet. It also assumes the client might have a more modest income and so perhaps cannot afford the more robust packages outlined in the second pricing structure.

1. The first pricing structure is to create a monthly salary for yourself while encouraging clients to show up and achieve their goals. If they don't show up, they lose money. The pricing structure in table 4 is based on the goal rate of sixty dollars per hour.

Sessions Per Week	Payment Schedule	Pricing Incentive	The Math	Notes
4	Monthly	2 free sessions	4 sessions x 4 weeks = 16 sessions 16 sessions x $60 = $960 total for the month	Including the 2 free sessions for paying up front, monthly brings your hourly rate to $55 per hour. However, this can normally be recouped as most clients will miss one or two sessions so the hourly rate is maintained at $60 per hour. It is up to you to negotiate price if the client wants to make up the missed sessions.
4	Bi-weekly	1/2 price on one session – or $30 off	4 sessions x 2 weeks = 8 sessions 8 sessions x $60 = $480 Bi-weekly $480 - $30 discount = $450 every two weeks	Bi-weekly means a check every other week so you will need to budget accordingly. Since they are paying every two weeks (28 days) and most months have 30-31 days, they do not receive the extra free sessions from paying monthly.
4	Weekly	No discount	4 sessions x 1 week = 4 sessions 4 x $60 = $240 total per week	Some clients simply cannot afford to pay monthly, but this could also be an indicator that they are not entirely ready to commit. Have a good cancellation (i.e., no refunds) policy in place the client has both read and signed.
4	Daily	No discount	1 session x $60 =	This is not a desirable training environment so use your best judgment. Again, have a good cancellation policy in place.
3	Monthly	2 free sessions	3 sessions x 4 weeks = 12 sessions 12 sessions x $65 = $780 total for the month	Including the 2 free sessions for paying up front, monthly brings your hourly rate to $56 per hour. However, this can normally be recouped as most clients will miss one or two sessions so the hourly rate is maintained at $65 per hour. It is up to you to negotiate price if the client wants to make up the missed sessions. Also, notice the $65 per hour rate. Adding $5 to the price may encourage the client to consider the 4 sessions per week package (whereby they would save $80 because the price per session is $60 versus the $65).
3	Bi-weekly	1/2 price on one session – or $30 off	3 sessions x 2 weeks = 6 sessions 6 sessions x $65 = $390 Bi-weekly $390 - $30 discount = $360 every two weeks	Bi-weekly means a check every other week so you will need to budget accordingly. Since they are paying every two weeks (28 days) and most months have 30-31 days, they do not receive the extra free sessions from paying monthly.
3	Weekly	No discount	3 sessions x 1 week = 3 sessions 4 x $65 = $260 per week	Some clients simply cannot afford to pay monthly, but this could also be an indicator that they are not entirely ready to commit. Have a good cancellation (i.e., no refunds) policy in place the client has both read and signed.
3	Daily	No discount	1 session x $65 = $65 per session	This is not a desirable training environment so use your best judgment. Again, have a good cancellation policy in place.

Table 4.

Here is further explanation of table 4:

- Buy four sessions per week.
  - Those who pay monthly receive two free sessions.
    - Four sessions times four weeks equals sixteen sessions. Sixteen sessions times $60 per session equals $960 per month.
    - This pricing structure assumes that a typical month with thirty days potentially has eighteen sessions. If clients pay monthly, they receive a discount on the price per session. The trick here is that most clients will miss two, three, or four sessions per month, leaving you with more money in your pocket for less work. Since it is their fault they missed sessions, they will be okay with the resulting pricing.
  - Those who pay biweekly receive a half-session discount of thirty dollars off the total price.
  - Those who pay weekly get no discount. (Be sure to have a firm cancellation policy.)
  - Those who pay per session get no discount. (Be sure to have a firm cancellation policy.)
- Buy three sessions per week.
  - Those who pay monthly receive one or two free sessions.
    - Three sessions times four weeks equals twelve sessions. Twelve sessions times $65 per session equals $780 per month.
    - Adding $5 to the price encourages clients to buy the four-sessions-per-week package. Also, this price assumes that a typical month with thirty days typically potentially has thirteen or fourteen sessions. If clients pay monthly, they receive a

discount on the price per session. Again, the trick is they will miss two to three sessions per month, leaving you with more money in your pocket for less work. Since it is their fault they missed sessions, they will be okay with the resulting pricing.
- Those who pay biweekly get a half-session discount of thirty dollars off the total price.
- Those who pay weekly get no discount. (Be sure to have a firm cancellation policy.)
- Those who pay per session get no discount. (Be sure to have a firm cancellation policy.)

- Buy two sessions or a single session per week.
  - Those who pay monthly get no sessions free and pay seventy-five dollars per session. Increasing the price per session by ten dollars encourages the previous packages.
  - Those who pay biweekly get no discount. (Be sure to include a firm cancellation policy.)
  - Those who pay weekly get no discount. (Be sure to include a firm cancellation policy.)
  - Those who pay per session get no discount. (Be sure to include a firm cancellation policy.)

2. The second pricing structure is large packages. Based on the number of sessions per week that you are targeting, you can create packages that reflect the time lines needed to achieve certain goals. Offer a discount to your clients if they buy bigger packages. I am targeting three sessions per week for this example. The fees are up front and paid in full, and they are designed to encourage clients to move up the ladder from buying twelve sessions at seventy-five dollars per session to buying a package of forty-eight sessions at sixty dollars per session. In all cases, have

a firm cancellation policy in place that the client has read and signed.

Package	Per Session Rate	Duration	The Math
48 Session	$60	4 Months	48 sessions x $60 = $2,880
36 Session	$65	3 Months	36 sessions x $65 = $2,340
24 Session	$70	2 Months	24 sessions x $70 = $1,680
12 Session	$75	1 Month	12 sessions x $75 = $900

Table 5.

Here is a further explanation of table 5:

- Buy a forty-eight-session package.
  - Sixty dollars per session times forty-eight sessions equals $2,880.
  - This package contains four months of training at the best price of sixty dollars per session. This is the target package for a person with a long-term goal.
- Buy a thirty-six-session package.
  - Sixty-five dollars per session times thirty-six sessions equals $2,340.
  - This package contains three months of training at five dollars more per sessions than the forty-eight session package. This encourages clients to buy the larger package, as it is a better deal.
- Buy a twenty-four-session package.
  - Twenty-four sessions times $70 per session equals $1,680.
  - This package contains two months of training for another five dollars more per session. This encourages clients to buy either of the previous packages.

- Buy a twelve-session package.
  - Twelve sessions times $75 per session equals $900.
  - This package contains one month of training at the highest per-session rate, which encourages clients to buy all of the previous packages.

With both of these pricing structures, I am encouraging a larger commitment by making the potential client the best deal. There are other ways to develop pricing, but these are the most commonly used because they are the most effective. Charging someone per session is less optimal due to the constant exchange of credit card information, checks, or cash. Charging per session also discourages longer-term commitment from the client, which is bad for both parties as the client will not be able to achieve his or her goal.

There are a few other ideas that can assist the client in committing to a longer training time. Let's say a client is struggling to buy a package or commit to a monthly fee. For people who are struggling to buy, it is important to make sure you still get the sales by encouraging them with add-ons. Below is a list of add-ons that may entice clients to buy your premium package. Be aware that some require more time or have less net profit but can help forward clients' goals and build more value into the sale:

- include a free supplement that you recommend
- add a free nutritional program
- include a free grocery-store trip
- include a food-preparation course with an in-home cooking lesson and instructions on how to prepare meals
- allow clients to bring friends to the training sessions with similar goals and split the cost
- add one or two more free sessions to a package
- include another free service, such as a gym membership, a massage, or a beauty service

Add-ons are all meant to entice the buyer to complete the purchase. To further bait the potential client you can also make the sale appear time sensitive by adding wording such as, "If you purchase today, I can include" or "These are available for a limited time." When you present these packages with supreme confidence, your likelihood to close the sale increases, although there are other factors that can affect the sale.

Identifying Reasons People Don't Buy

Transitioning a client at the end of a free session toward a sale is one of the most confusing areas for most personal trainers. How do you get someone to say "yes, I am in" and process his or her payment? All of the previous sections have prepared you for this moment. Did you build enough value? Did you pitch the product that best meets the client's needs? Does the client have any concerns that you left unaddressed? Since we know why people buy, let's look at reasons why people don't buy:

- Fear of failure: Sometimes, the fear of failure alone will dissuade people from purchasing, as they are safe from failure if they do not try. You address this barrier when attempting to build the emotional connection. When clients' thoughts of accomplishment outweigh their fears of failure, you have successfully attached positive emotions to your service, giving them more inclination to buy.
- Low perceived value: You didn't build enough value in the presentation to make the purchaser believe the product is worth the money. Building value throughout your presentation is crucial. You must convince buyers they need your services in order to reach their fitness goals.
- Money: Quite simply, if you have approached a potential client who truly does not have the means to purchase,

then the sale will be impossible. It is important to find that out as soon as possible rather than expend a lot of time and effort during the course of conversation. Try to build in questions about where clients work, live, and so forth without being too upfront or personal.
- Failure to ask: The most important thing you can do is ask for the sale. Do not forget to include the call to action in your sales presentation.
- Lack of proof: The client does not believe that what you are selling will work. When you are selling something that is not tangible—personal training—it is important to prove to your client that their results will come. You can do this with testimonials or stories about your other clients' results.

Although there are many reasons why people don't buy personal-training packages, those in the list above are the most common. It is important to understand these reasons when you meet with a potential client; if you ensure that you recognize and avoid them, sales will be more likely to close.

Identifying Barriers and Creating Solutions
When you identify a barrier to purchasing training, it needs to be noted and addressed in the final closing segment of the free assessment or training session. If you miss a barrier during the initial stages of the interview, you will not be able to create a solution, making the sale less likely to occur. I've listed the most common barriers to exercising or working with a personal trainer:

- Time: I don't have the time to work out.
- Money: I don't have enough money to purchase training.
- Injury: I would work out, but my knee hurts when I do.
- Low energy: I am so exhausted after work I can't bring myself to go to the gym.

- Lack of need: I know what I'm doing in the gym. I mean, look at me.
- Need for approval from the financer: I need to see if purchasing this is okay with my husband.
- Belief that exercise is not fun or enjoyable: Running on a treadmill is boring.
- Belief that exercise is ineffective: No matter how much I exercise, I just can't lose weight.

You can find barriers by asking the power questions listed in chapter five Asking questions to uncover clients' true motivations behind their goals or actions is called digging or root-cause analysis. When you identify a barrier, it is your job as the trainer to create a solution to that barrier. Here is a list of examples for how to address each barrier:

- Time: Time, along with money, is one of the most common barriers you will see in the field. There are a few ways to address the barrier of time. One way is to discuss the importance of exercise and how time should be made to do it. Another way is to get an hourly breakdown of the client's daily schedule, analyze it, and assist him or her to make thirty to sixty minutes available to exercise.
- Money: Financial barriers can be addressed in several ways. One of them is to create money within a client's current budget by analyzing some basic spending information. Start by asking how many times per week the client eats out. Usually, it is somewhere around ten times, as buying one lunch per day and dinner a few times a week is easy to achieve. When I explain to my clients that each time they eat out it equates to around fifteen dollars, I can teach them that cooking their own food is not only healthier but can also save them about one hundred dollars per week. They will be eating healthier to achieve

their goals and saving money, which they will spend with you, the personal trainer. As an incentive, you could offer a free in-home food-preparation session to encourage clients sign up for a larger package.

- Injury: Injuries should be one of the easiest barriers to overcome, as clients cannot exercise by themselves without pain. Take the client through a pain-free workout and then explain how the personal-training sessions can address the injury and lessen or eliminate the pain. Selling to an injury can be easy, especially if you are knowledgeable about posture and joint positioning around the affected area; if not, do your research.
- Low energy: Low energy, otherwise known as laziness, can be seen as a lack of motivation. Your job is to motivate and convince clients that working out together will increase their daily energy levels and bring back their desires to exercise. One of the reasons they are in front of a trainer is because they are out of shape and have not made any effort. Starting with a personal trainer will prove that they can put in the needed effort.
- Lack of need: "So you're Brad Pitt. That don't impress me much," said Shaniya Twain in that song, which will now be stuck in your head for days. There are two ways to approach this type of client. One way is to show them their imperfections in flexibility, image, or posture, and the other is to explain to them how even the best personal trainers need personal trainers. Maybe potential clients are stuck in the same boring routines and need to mix things up. Explain periodization and how it could take them to their next levels. Everyone benefits from having a trainer as an outsider's perspective can enhance the attainability of any goal.

- Need for approval from the financer: For clients who are not the financial decision-makers in their families, as the fitness professional, try to communicate with whoever can make a decision via phone or e-mail. Or, if the potential client does have some funds at his or her discretion, sell to what he or she can comfortably invest.
- Belief that exercise is not fun or enjoyable: Your ability to sell new, fun, and exciting forms of exercise will benefit you greatly for this barrier. Use the power question that asks about the client's previous experience with exercise, and respond to this belief. When you know what clients have tried, you can discuss how different types of training will free them from boredom. Include a bit of science around the benefits of resistance training to increase credibility and trust.
- Belief that exercise in ineffective: So the potential client hasn't had success at exercising because his or her thirty-minute at-home elliptical session twice a week is not cutting it. Find out what potential clients have tried, and explain how your programming can break their plateaus and get them moving in the right direction.

Recognizing barriers and creating unique ways to address them will be one of the most important aspects to selling people who are on the fence. If you leave barriers unaddressed, they will most likely prevent you from closing the sale. Grab a friend, and role play. Practicing will create competency at selling to these barriers.

Sales Stories
When used appropriately, telling a sales story can be great for the sales environment. Stories can build trust and credibility and

enhance the buying atmosphere. In order to understand how to use a story in selling, you must first define the components of the story you are telling.

The story should contain these elements:

1. a previous client
2. the same goal or similar barrier to that of the person you are telling the story to
3. a positive outcome about how someone overcame an obstacle and achieved a goal

For example, the potential client in front of you is discussing being so tired after work that she hasn't been making it to the gym. You say, "I had a previous client dealing with the same issue. She was a lawyer and worked twelve- to fourteen-hour days. She would come to me for a quick session after she left the office. Although she battled fatigue for the first few sessions, her energy levels quickly skyrocketed. She was able to sleep better, and the hormonal changes from her improved nutrition and the exercise were able to make those hours that she put into her work more productive. I really think that you would have a similar experience, as you mentioned having the same lack of energy."

What this story does is create empathy with her situation and a sense of understanding, while at the same time offering her a solution to her barrier. If she truly wants to achieve her goal, she will accept the solution you have created for her, especially after you have reinforced its success with the story.

You may wonder what to do if you don't have a story that meets the needs of every particular client's barrier or goal. I don't recommend straightforward lying, but rearranging small details to meet different clients' needs can make each story more relevant.

Creating Closing Sales Statements

It is officially decision time for the potential client; you have built an abundance of value, and all that remains is to close the sale. You have taken note of all of the suggestions in this book, your client has no further questions or concerns, and all you need to do is swipe the credit card. This section features unique closing styles and statements that will secure your sales. Understand that any of these techniques can be used with confidence, but based on your sales personality, one may align with you more:

- The direct close: This method of closing relays the thought that you believe the sale is already a done deal, leaving little room for the client to back out. Use caution, as this method has the potential to scare people away who are undecided about committing. Here are the statements that align with the direct-closing technique:
  - When would you like to schedule your first session?
  - Shall we get started?
  - Can we proceed with the payment options?
- The indirect close or the no close: This method is a slightly more passive approach that allows the client to feel as if he or she is in control. If you are looking to maintain as much trust as possible, according to a study performed by Hawes and Winick (1996), "The highest ranking mean score for prospect trust occurred in the 'no-close' scenario." Because this method increases client comfort, it's a great place to start if you are new to selling. The statements below reflect the no-close or indirect-closing technique:
  - How do you feel about getting started, since if we focus, we can reach your fitness goal in three months?

- Are you ready to take the next step toward enhancing your health and fitness?
- Is what we discussed today something you would want to pursue?
- The pros-and-cons close: This close is a great way to transition a client into thinking about purchasing. When the pros far outweigh the cons, the client can see the value and the benefit to starting with a personal trainer. Be sure to include the emotional connection and the small details that prove you were closely listening. The pros-and-cons chart can look like this:

Pros	Cons
- have more energy - look good naked - feel better - sleep better - be able to outlast little Jimmy at soccer practice - reduce tough stress from job - prove to Derek I can easily lose thirty pounds	- miss out on thirty minutes of family time, but enjoy our time together more because I feel better and am less tired - spend more money, but feeling, looking, and being healthy are priceless. Plus, I save money by eating out less often—win-win. - could fail, but remember trainer is here to guide you every step of the way, and trainer knows you will be successful working together. - worsen injury, but trainer has worked with people with the same injury and seen amazing results in short time frames. Plus, trainer knows a ton of exercises that will not cause any pain.

Note that the cons list should be filled with barriers and fears about exercise. It should also include the solutions created to beat those barriers.

- The hard close: This method of closing tends to push the client toward the purchase by using fear or scare tactics. This is an aggressive, albeit effective, way to close, but I don't recommend it unless it truly is in your personality. Some people do need that extra push or different perspective to snap them into gear, but use caution as you may not only lose the sale but also leave a sour taste for both parties:
    - Considering how effective exercise is at reducing the risk of cancer, it is probably best to get started as soon as possible.
    - Since you will continue to feel bad about the way you look unless you do something about it, the person in the mirror is asking you to start today.
    - Considering what might happen if you don't start training with me, let's start working together. (Yep, you would probably die.)
    - Because the sale on personal training is ending today, I wouldn't be able to get you the same price if you wait.
    - If I make this sale today, I would be the number-one trainer in the club. Would you help me achieve that title?
    - Since it is never too soon to change your life for the better, are you willing to do that?
- Two-option or multiple-option close: This technique forces the client to consider and hopefully choose one of the options you've laid out on the table. It is a little presumptuous and should be used with caution, but it can be a great way to transition to the close:
    - Would you like to train three or four times per week?
    - Which package do you think would work best for you?

- Would you rather pay monthly or biweekly?
- Where would you like to train—your house, the gym, or at my in-home gym?
- No-more-barriers close: This type of close proves there is no reason why the client should not purchase, because you have addressed all the barriers and objections:
  - Is there anything about training that you are still unsure of?
  - Is there any reason you think you should not start training today?
  - Why shouldn't you start training?

Here are other tips to remember throughout your process of closing the sale and beyond:

- Remember that "your foundation includes being able to speak clearly, colorfully, and persuasively—the closer's fundamental tools. And this applies in any selling interaction. If you're not an expert speaker, start studying. You must master the language" (Roth 2002, 11).
- Don't do all the talking. The best way to close a sale is to listen to your client, adapt, and then react to what he or she is saying.
- Stay confident throughout the process. Nine out of ten sales attempts fail, so do not get discouraged—it will show during your current attempt and push the client away.
- Follow up with clients every other week after closing sales to make sure they are satisfied with the training process and that they are happy with their progress. You must always remember that with every session, you are still selling their next package. Discuss long-term goals, and genuinely listen to what they like to talk about most. There is

no reason why a client should not continue training with you, especially if the experience is enjoyable.

Being Sure Clients Don't Leave Without Your Help

So, you did everything you could, but the client is still not purchasing one of your training packages. What happens next? It is your job as a health-and-fitness professional to do everything you can to help others, so don't let anyone leave without getting help. You have shown the client all of your packages that include training, but what about the packages that don't? Below is a list of ways you can continue trying to receive someone's business after the attempt to sell training has fallen through:

- Online training: For a set monthly fee of $150, the client receives a weekly workout program including all exercise variables, a nutritional plan, and a weekly or daily check-in via e-mail or phone. (Throw in one session per month for $250 per month total). Online training entails designing templates, shopping lists, and nutritional guides and giving the client access to an exercise library (for examples, visit the "Exercises" page of Bodybuilding.com or EXRX.net) for optimal understanding. Online training is less effective, as the benefit of meeting with a trainer goes far beyond exercise instructions on paper. However, it is a good way to increase your profitability by meeting the budgets of more individuals. You need to let people know that without taking help, they are choosing to live the same lifestyles they have been, which will reinforce their current or worsening states of health.
- Three-month workout program: Having a set program that will get people to a general goal, such as weight loss

or muscle gain, is a great tool to create last-minute sales. Offering this program for fifty to one hundred dollars, or more, will set clients up with some basic guidelines as to what they can do in the gym without a trainer. You can also bundle this program with your nutritional guide and sell the package for more. This program does not include a monthly fee, so it could be less intimidating for the financially unstable client.

- Nutritional guide: You should have created nutritional guides for your clients already, so selling one for twenty to thirty dollars as a last-ditch effort to close a sale should be easy. As already mentioned, a guide can be paired with a workout program to benefit the customer more and increase your profitability. A sample nutritional guide can be found at BalancedBites.com.

- Boot camp or group-training program: Inviting a reluctant one-on-one client to participate in your boot-camp or group-training sessions can be a great way to generate income. For the price of ten to twenty dollars per person, clients can still achieve their goals by joining your group classes. Make sure you have flyers available with your schedules and prices, as well your website where details about the classes can be found. You might also consider suggesting a package of ten group sessions.

With each attempt at creating and closing the sale, you have truly proven that you have done everything you can to help individuals achieve their fitness goals. If you follow through with all of these efforts with confidence, your conversion percentage is bound to increase.

Conclusion

This guide has taken you through the process for growing your personal-fitness clientele: gaining certifications, doing outreach, validating your fitness theory, finding your niche, creating marketing materials, learning how to build up your sales, breaking down barriers, putting together packages, and being positive.

Your ability to learn and grow comes from having passion for what you seek to understand. As a personal trainer, that passion is connected to helping others live the most physically fit, healthy, and enjoyable lives possible. Nothing can compare to the feeling a trainer gets when clients are completely transformed into the healthy and happy people they've always wanted to become.

Being trainers allows us to make money by teaching people how to grow in happiness while shrinking their waistlines. Students of sales are able to help more people get to this happiness, as they have the abilities to convert more prospects into clients. Although a trainer may only have 15-20 clients, a personal trainer's ability to have a positive impact on the lives of others is immeasurable, and having a positive impact is one of the most important things a human can do. Go out, and apply everything you have learned from this book with the genuine intention of helping people grow in health and happiness by looking good, feeling good, and loving themselves more. As Ben Franklin said, "Nothing ventured; nothing gained." If you don't make an effort, nothing will change.

References

Brehm, B. 2004. *Successful Fitness Motivation Strategies.* Champaign: Human Kinetics.

Dalgic, T. and M. Leeuw 1994. "Niche Marketing Revisited: Concept, Applications and Some European Cases." *European Journal of Marketing* 28: 39–55.

Hawes, J. Strong and B. J. Winick. 1996. "Do Closing Techniques Diminish Prospect Trust?" *Industrial Marketing Management* 25: 349–360.

Raghunathan, R. and S. C. Huang. 2009. *Post-Hoc Rationalization: Affect-Based Post-Decisional Revision of Attribute Importance.* 1–12.

Robinette, S. et al. 2000. "The Hallmark Way of Winning Customers for Life." *Emotion Marketing*: 3–4.

Roth, C. 2002. "Secrets to Closing Sales." *Audio-Tech Business Book* 10: 5–11

Tauber, E. 1972. "Why Do People Shop?" *Journal of Marketing* 36: 46–47.

Do you need Continuing Education Units or Credits? (CEUs, CECs)

The Business and Sales: The Guide to Success as a Personal Trainer is now available online at www.fitnessmentors.com/business-and-sales-ceu-course/ . Visit the link or call today (424) 675-0476 to reserve your 2.0* CEUs and recertify your personal training certification.

Approved for CECs from the following companies:
NASM, NESTA, ACE, ACSM, NSCA,
AFAA, ISSA, NCCPT

*Number of CECs varies by certifying body.

Made in the USA
Middletown, DE
01 March 2018